Intimate
Partners

Other Books by the Author

Rekindling the Spirit in Work

Jupiter's Rings: Balance From the Inside Out

Intimate Partners

Howard Joel Schechter, Ph.D.

BARRYTOWN
STATION HILL

Published by Barrytown/Station Hill Press, Inc. in Barrytown, New York 12507, as a project of the Institute for Publishing Arts, Inc., in Barrytown, New York, a not-for-profit, tax-exempt organization [501(c)(3)], supported in part by grants from the New York State Council on the Arts.

E-mail: publishers@stationhill.org
Online catalogue: http://www.stationhill.org

Cover and interior design by Susan Quasha

Library of Congress Cataloging-in-Publication Data

Schechter, Howard, 1945-
 Intimate partners / Howard Joel Schechter.
     p. cm.
 ISBN 978-1-58177-109-1 (alk. paper)
 1. Intimacy (Psychology) I. Title.

 BF575.I5S33 2008
 158.2—dc22

                                          2008028358

Printed in the United States of America

To my brother Neal

If life is a school, relationship is its university.

EVA PIERRAKOS

Contents

1 ❧ Overview

The elixir is hidden in the poison.
RUMI

I have been in almost continuous long-term intimate relationship since I began going steady with Judy Levin in the 7th grade. Still, I never would have had the courage to begin relationship work without a strong push from the outside. That push, or perhaps it was a pull, came to my wife Barbara and me from our friends Marlene and John Adair. They had been participants in a workshop, on another topic, which we lead at Esalen Institute in Big Sur, California. They invited us to lead a group they had organized in Modesto, California, and because the participants were couples, we assumed the topic was relationship. We later learned we were wrong in that assumption—John and Marlene's intention had been for us to select the topic of our choice. However, since we believed it was meant to be on couples, we swallowed hard and decided to challenge ourselves, agreeing to lead a workshop on "Intimate Relationship."

Although we got into the work "by mistake," what is crystal clear to us now is that it was no mistake at all: it was our calling. The work has become our passion, and our life together has been a laboratory for this learning. A line from a Grateful Dead song—"What a long strange trip it's been"—describes our subsequent journey with couples work. This book is about what we have learned from the many couples we have worked with. It is simultaneously a kind of joint biography of our life together. The work Barbara and I do—both on our own relationship, and with the couples we guide—has enriched our bond and our lives enormously. It has been one of the great learning experiences of my life.

At first this work presented some significant challenges to our relationship, and from time to time it still does. The disturbance occurs as we try our best to live up to a level of quality that the old Chinese sages might call the "superior" relationship. The demands of integrity require that we "walk our talk"—that is, that we live the principles we teach. In so doing, we are required to shine light into the dark corners of relationship, those places we tend to avoid, and the avoidance of which prevents us from realizing the full potential of our joy. Barbara and I do a pretty good job of nurturing our connection overall, though sometimes we slip and spill and make a mess. The falls teach us humility, and reinforce the knowledge that developing intimate relationship is a never-ending process. We have learned an enormous amount in these past 20 years of focusing our attention on intimate partnership.

This book is about the development and nurturance of mature committed relationship. It is an attempt to illuminate the principles that allow the creation of what we sometimes call the *Healing Relationship*: a relationship of such high-quality connection that it creates an atmosphere of mutual support in which both partners can heal from the emotional wounds they carry into adulthood, so that they might live up to their vast potential as unique human beings. Romantic love, as we will later see, is but an opening, a doorway into the more developed and evolved bond we call *Mature Love*. Though we may aspire to this kind of relationship, our actions often do not produce the desired outcome. This points to the Buddha's observation that we hate suffering, but love its causes. That is, we desire to be happy, to have harmonious intimate relationship, but we continue to choose behaviors that make the relationship, and therefore ourselves, unhappy.

The two basic ways relationships are formed and sustained is through *doing* together and *talking* together. This book focuses a good deal of attention on the second factor, communication. Communication is the tool in intimate relationship that can both keep us out of trouble, and extricate us once we have stepped into it. My hope is that the guidance in this book, both attitudinal and skill-focused, will help intimate partners live a more harmonious and joyful life together.

Many authors have expressed the belief that intimate relationship is a practice: a path to personal healing, growth, and spiritual development. I agree completely. Through relationship we are given the opportunity to heal emotional wounds based in personal history that restrict our freedom of choice and action in the present, keeping us stuck in dysfunctional and unpleasant patterns. When we are not in relationship, though we may experience the discomfort of loneliness, we are not challenged with seeing ourselves constantly mirrored back by our partner. Relationship relentlessly demands that we look at our unfinished business because we project our wounded parts onto our partner, then see them reflected back to us. Interestingly, this phenomenon is phonetically embedded in the word intimacy itself: "into-me-I-see." The gift of this ever-present process of projection is that it enables us more quickly to integrate the rejected parts of ourselves and move toward wholeness. When we live outside of intimate relationship, we can escape this challenging fate. But we also miss the magnificent opportunity it presents.

Having our unintegrated parts mirrored back to us is difficult, and at times feels just too uncomfortable to handle. In those times the tendency is to run away from the struggle. But the more skillful and effective behavior is to *lean into* it, as we would a strong wind—to really feel the feelings and mine the teachings within them. As the writer Francisco de Ossuna eloquently stated, "Do not believe that the battle of love is like other fights. Its arrows and blows are gifts and blessings." If we can learn to see the challenges of intimate relationship as opportunities for our healing and growth, then we can more easily welcome these difficulties, in much the way that a runner welcomes the ache in her legs as a sign that she is making herself stronger. With this knowledge we can progressively learn the attitudes and skills to positively handle the challenges, rather than viewing them as the bitter price of companionship. When conflict and unkindness are reduced, what we discover lying naturally just beneath the surface are harmony and joy. This joy derives from an inherent satisfaction in the sense of completion that comes with intimate relationship.

It appears that one of the primary reasons intimate relationship is so fulfilling is that it satisfies a deep need within us, perhaps a biologically hardwired drive for connection. As animals—and pack animals at that—we humans feel a sense of completion from connection with others of our kind, particularly with a mate. Since we are also spiritual creatures, this may mimic the drive to unite with the Divine. This process of uniting with another and honoring the divinity within them ignites the awareness of divinity within oneself.

Carl Jung, one of the greatest psychological thinkers of all time, believed strongly in this drive for completion. He posited that we all have both male and female aspects within us to varying degrees, but that the dominant aspect, which forms the basis of our gender identity, is completed by coming together with someone who represents the opposite gender. This is the origin of the concept of *soul mate*. For someone with a predominantly male gender identity (often, though not necessarily, a man), his soul is completed when he unites with someone who personifies his inner female (often, though not necessarily, a woman), and vice versa.[1] Those of us in intimate relationship are blessed with a precious gift, one that has the potential to be the most important element in supporting a joyful life. It would be wise for us to value and treat intimate relationship as such, particularly knowing that the hand of fate can take this gift away from us at any moment. We are blessed when we have the offering of another person's companionship. We do not need to climb a mountain or plumb the oceans to find meaning in life. It is right here, standing by our side, living life with us.

2 ❦ Potential

It seems to me that true love is a discipline.
W.B. YEATS

*I*ntimate relationship can be the source of great joy, a way into personal growth and emotional healing. It can also be the source of deep suffering. It is frustrating to know how much joy relationship can bring, yet to see the frequency with which we turn it into suffering. The intention of this book is to help cultivate the joy of intimate relationship, and to show how to turn its painful aspects into an ally of personal development.

The benefits associated with becoming more skillful in the ways of relationship are many. Because the quality of an intimate relationship has such a profound impact on the quality of one's life, any improvement in it offers great leverage in positively affecting our personal happiness. Additionally, by liberating our energy from chronic conflict, we can reap great rewards in other aspects of our lives, such as work and health.

All of this presupposes the *willingness* to prioritize intimate relationship as an area of life that deserves focus, study, and effort. Because intimate relationship is so familiar, like the water we swim in, we tend to give it too little constructive attention. We expect that if we are "in love," it should all work out. Unfortunately, too often it doesn't. What is required is willingness: willingness to change our habitual and unconscious forms of relating. Experimenting with different and more consciously constructed attitudes and behavior results in benefits for the quality of one's relationship and one's life.

The entry gate to intimate relationship in our culture is generally determined by the process we call "falling in love." "Romantic love," while being an incredibly strong force in igniting relationship, is not sufficiently powerful to sustain a high quality intimate relationship over time. Many jokes are made in our culture about the barrenness of marriage as the years roll on. This attitude points to the insufficiency of romantic love to sustain a relationship, and to the lack of understanding about what does foster intimacy as a relationship matures.

One key to growing intimacy in relationship is a focus on *purpose*. The purpose of intimate relationship is a combination of factors, which vary for different people and different couples. My image for representing purpose in intimate relationship is that of two people walking hand-in-hand down the same path toward similar destinations. The highest form of intimate relationship, in my view, occurs when the partners walk side-by-side toward personal growth, spiritual awakening, and the joy of companionship.

As we will emphasize throughout the book, one of relationship's greatest gifts, and at the same time one of its most challenging aspects, is the mirroring that it provides. It is in the very nature of partnership that both our dark and light aspects are reflected back to us by the other. We can see ourselves in the other in ways we cannot without that reflection. If this process is handled in a mutually supportive and loving way, we can learn to accept both our greatness and our faults in a manner that would be inaccessible to us without the mirror of the intimate other. In a general sense, on our own we often do not know what state we are in emotionally and mentally. We simply swim in familiar inner waters. In partnership, our moods, behavior, attitudes, energy, and other not-yet-conscious feelings and states of mind are bounced back to us through our partner's experience of us.

The process of projection—that is, casting one's own attributes, feelings, or attitudes onto other people—usually demonstrates the parts of ourselves we have rejected, but are now ready to accept. We are cued to the presence of this possibility by noticing our reactivity to that quality in the other. Our strong reaction to our partner's lack of confidence, for example, is almost certainly an indication of some unresolved issue we have with ourselves around confidence. By seeing this in the other, we are presented with the opportunity to see and heal our own self-rejection.

Another way to look at the purpose of intimate relationship is to define it as a *growth practice*. That is, to view it as practice in much the way that meditation and yoga are spiritual practices, or that running is a physical practice. Relationship can be seen as a process one devotes oneself to in order to grow emotionally, mentally, and spiritually. John Wellwood, a student of relationship, expresses it well when he says, "For many of us today intimate relationship has become the new wilderness that brings us face to face with our gods and demons. When we approach it in this way intimacy becomes a path ... an unfolding process of personal and spiritual development." In my experience, those who reap the greatest benefit and joy from relationship are those who do approach it as a practice. This means demonstrating a devotion to the path of intimacy, a willingness to give it ample attention, and a commitment to working diligently to learn all that it has to teach.

One of the great gifts of intimate partnership is the possibility it offers to create a Healing Relationship. Within intimate partnership the possibility for healing old emotional wounds is enormous. It can create the conditions for a healing that fosters more openness within, and an ability to be and behave in the present without carrying the limits of old history into our actions. Intimate partnership does more than any other structural condition in our lives to facilitate the kind of healing that enables us to make choices rather than to remain tethered to unproductive habitual reactions. Because intimate relationship pushes so many of our emotional buttons, the surfacing of old wounds for healing makes it possible to restore ourselves to a more empowered state.

The Healing Relationship consists mainly of four elements, which I discuss in depth later in the book. The first of these is what I call the *U-Turn*. This is an approach to interpersonal conflict aimed at turning friction into learning by taking responsibility for our feelings and the reactions we direct at our partner. The second is cultivating *Emotional Wisdom*, which entails seeking to gain insight, understanding, and growth by inquiring deeply into the feelings generated by the day-to-day process of intimate relationship. The third is the practice of *Gratitude and Kindness* toward our partner for making this life journey with us, for sharing the joys and supporting us through the difficulties life inevitably brings. The fourth and final element is the practice of *Skillful Communication*, which involves learning the attitudes and behaviors that allow for clear, direct, open, and honest communication, helping us both to avoid and to resolve conflict.

If we practice these approaches to intimate relationship, our individual lives will inevitably grow richer, deeper, and more meaningful, while our relationship with our partner blossoms as a source of mutual delight. Making this effort goes beyond our own healing to serve as a model and inspiration to others, for whom the Healing Relationship can serve as a beacon and a model for peace.

When we consider that grammatically the word 'relationship' is a noun, we can see the source of some of the problems in intimate relationship. A noun is a fixed thing, a done deal, an article like a car or a coat. But relationship is better understood as a verb, a process that implies action and change over time. As a verb, it contains movement rather than an arrived at, finished thing. When we say "intimate relationship," if we think "intimate relating," an ongoing set of evolutionary changes over time, it is easier to accept the challenges it brings.

Every relationship is unique, and generalizations have their limitations. Orthodoxy of any kind can be stifling. Therefore, it is important to say that the ideas presented here are offerings, not dogma. They are pointers to help us discover our own unique truth, through our own unique experience as individuals and as couples. The perspective is not scientific in the strict sense of the word, in that it is not quantitatively based using a randomly selected sample population upon which we have tested and measured the correctness of a set of hypotheses. It is, however, empirically based. It is built upon the foundation of observation and the experiment of our own lives, as well as those of the many couples we have worked with. It is predicated upon what Ralph Waldo Emerson called "direct experience."

The emphasis is on the internal and psychological more than the external and sociological, and on the way in which we create our environment more than the influence of the environment upon us. The internal and external are, of course, linked. And it goes without saying that external social and economic dynamics have a significant effect on the quality of our lives and our relationships. Variables such as class, status, gender, race, and sexual orientation impact us and our relationships greatly. While history and society may define and limit the parameters of our experience, the power of the way we think and feel has enormous potential to improve the quality of our relationships within these parameters. No matter what our place in society, and no matter what our geographic position on the globe, the quality of our inner organization profoundly influences the quality of our outer experience of life. One only need look at the contented street dweller in India and compare him to the stressed-out, discontented American millionaire for proof of that.

I think of personal healing and growth work as analogous to the shape of the classical yin-yang symbol of Eastern philosophy. One half of the circle is in the light and one half is in the shadow, which suggests that to experience continuous growth in this life we are required to work both in the shadow and in the light. We expand our connection to the light through an ongoing process of perfecting our spiritual, mental, emotional, and physical being. And we learn the lessons inherent in the difficulties and pain of the shadow aspects of life. We do so by honoring, paying attention to, and inquiring deeply into the psychological material that is contained within the suffering of this life. Shadow material is a great teacher, as it is most often a matter of the unconscious bringing to our attention what we need to learn in order to be whole in the present.

3 ⁘ Relationship is Nested in Life

Relationship *can* be understood as being nested within the greater container of our lives. We need to choose a partner and nurture a relationship that support the life we want, rather than allowing our lives to be a series of reactions to the dynamics presented by relationship. The quality of this one precious life ought to be our primary concern. Relationship should support the life we want, not vice versa. Too often the situation is reversed: our life is nested in relationship, and our life becomes a reaction to the interactional dynamics of the association.

Often people enter into relationship based on reasons having little to do with what will actually fulfill their lives. We generally choose a relationship as a response to a process we call "falling in love." Our life then becomes a reflection of that relationship. In this circumstance, our life is nested in our relationship. It is more an image of an adaptation than a consciously constructed partnership that supports the life we would like to live. When we enter intimate partnership only because we are "in love," then we may be creating a win-lose opposition between Life and Love. It may turn into choosing for love at the expense of choosing for life. It would be far better to choose for both Love and Life. We can choose for both if we opt for a partner who can hold our hand and walk with us down a path toward a mutually satisfying destination. For me, that path leads in the direction of continuous liberation from conditioned limitations toward ongoing spiritual growth.

When we choose only for romantic love, incognizant of purpose, there is imminent danger that we may drift into the cliché relationship of boring flatness and "falling out of love." What is actually happening when this occurs is that the individuals and the relationship have lost direction.

The romance has become an insufficient compass. The partners are now being pushed largely by interactional dynamics, reacting, responding, and trying to keep from drowning in the stress and strain of attempting to bridge two roads going off in different directions into the woods.

This was the fate of an otherwise lovely young couple I worked with, Rena and Kenny. They fell in love and began to live together, hoping, as most couples do, to be together "until death do us part." As time passed it became clear that they were neither on the same path nor headed in the same direction. Rena wanted children, monogamy, and a quiet country life. Kenny did not want children, could not resist the attractions of other women, and longed for the excitement of urban action. Their relationship folded after a brief honeymoon period and three agonizing years of suffering. Some years later, Rena met a man with a different set of values, one that more closely matched her own. She and John now have two children, live in a lovely cabin in the woods, and by all reports are very happy.

Romantic love needs to open into Mature Love for intimate relationship to be satisfying and to endure. The essence of Mature Love consists of common values, playful companionship, and mutual support.

If intimate relationship is to nest in life rather than our experiencing life as driven by whatever interactional dynamics flow from the dice roll of romantic love, then we must seek to answer two basic questions:

1. What kind of life do we want?

2. What kind of relationship will support it?

Of course, we must answer these questions for ourselves based on our own unique nature. What is necessary, however, is at least to begin to answer them *before* entering into an intimate relationship if it is to be successful. This imperative highlights an important theme that is emphasized throughout the book: though we are focusing on relationship, it is the *individual* who is the true unit of inquiry. It is the individual who is growing and healing.

In fact, it is literally impossible to physically touch the entity we call relationship. It has no blood and guts. It is a nonmaterial construct.

Accordingly, the warm bodies engaged in the relationship are the central focus of this work—the ways we think, feel, and behave. Emphasis on the individual as the primary focus implies that we must concentrate on understanding and developing ourselves even as we consider entering into and participating in a satisfying intimate relationship. Only then are we in a position to be with a partner skillfully as we create the life we want.

Intimate relationship is a deeper, more developed, more mature matter than romantic attraction. It is certain to provide opportunities to feel the discomfort that the mirroring presents. Knowing that it will be difficult as well as joyful, we can more easily face the discomfort because we are not just enduring, we are creating the life we desire.

4 ⚭ Stay in Your Own Skin

We do not see things as they are, we see things as we are.
THE TALMUD

The first and perhaps most important principle of the Healing Relationship is taking full responsibility for what is happening inside our own skin. Nearly all relationship problems are individual problems arising in the context of the couple. Consequently, we need to own our thoughts and feelings, and not make them the responsibility of the other. Whatever it is that our partner says or does, we are the source of our own reactions.

Our partner cannot truly cause us to be angry, sad, hurt, or frustrated. Rather, their behavior, which we may be experiencing as unpleasant, serves as an impulse that triggers a set of thoughts and feelings within us. Those thoughts and feelings happen within us, not within the other; accordingly, they are our own responsibility. This simple and straightforward truth so often evades us when we are emotionally triggered.

The common response to our partner when they say or do something we find unpleasant is to blame them for "making us" feel bad. In reaction to having been blamed, our partner will typically withdraw or attack in return. Then we are locked in an unpleasant conflict arising from the initial false assumption that they were the source of our discomfort. Although they may have evoked our response, the reaction comes from us.

When we recognize that our feelings are playing out within us, the more skillful response to our discomfort when triggered by our partner is to take responsibility for what we think, feel, and do. This we call *Going Vertical*. When Barbara says or does something that elicits my reaction, my intention is first to go within, then vertically up and down inside myself to understand what is happening with me. I don't first go horizontally, out towards her, making her responsible for how I feel. The tendency in our culture is to go horizontal reactively: to focus outward toward the other, blaming them for our internal experience. Then it is common to try to change the other so that we can feel better.

If we learn first to go vertical, and only then to go horizontal by sharing our internal experience with our partner, we have the possibility of developing great intimacy. We first go within to understand our experience, and then go horizontal to communicate it to the other. This combination, in this order—initially owning our experience and trying more fully to understand it, then communicating our inner landscape to our partner—nourishes intimacy.

We are most likely first to go horizontal inappropriately at those times when a response to our partner's behavior evokes a big charge within us. That is, when we experience an outsized emotional reaction that is not proportional to the context and to the behavior that is actually unfolding. The big charge is a clear indicator that a sensitive place within us has been triggered, and that it is time to make a complete U-Turn. It is time to withdraw the horizontal energy, and to inquire gently and lovingly within ourselves. Otherwise, we are behaving more like experimental mice, reacting predictably when the stimulus is presented.

Going vertical requires that we slow down and not respond immediately like those laboratory mice. We slow ourselves and make an effort to become aware of our thoughts and feelings, noticing if any shift or openings arise out of this inner exploration. Behavior that emerges from a process of self-inquiry and understanding has greater integrity and tends to produce more skillful action and better outcomes in the real world.

Dependency in a relationship feeds the dysfunctional horizontal movement. Dependency creates merging with the other. When merging occurs, whatever you are feeling, I am feeling. When one partner is dependent, the other inevitably falls into some form of codependency as well. Dependency, codependency, and the anxiety they produce push the partners into losing their sense of center, their sense of what is objective and real, their sense of "true north." Under these conditions, each partner merges into the other, while neither takes responsibility for their own self. Going horizontal is the dominant mode of interaction, and real intimacy is threatened.

Perhaps the single most important thing I can do for the quality of my life and the quality of my relationship is to choose to fully own my own feelings and thoughts—even when it is really difficult, even when I do not want to, even when my fondest wish is to make my partner wrong. Even *then* I need to own it.

5 ❧ Don't Try to Change Your Partner

Those who see themselves as whole make no demands.
A COURSE IN MIRACLES

All suffering is based on attachment and craving.
THE BUDDHA

A provocative statement related to the "stay in your own skin" theme, and another excellent guideline in intimate relationship, is "never try to change the other person about anything, ever." Optimally, change comes from within the other as a gift based upon a response to our stated wants and needs, not as the result of a demand, coercion, or manipulation.

The effort to change our partner from how they are to how we want them to be is highly destructive to intimacy. Allowing and accepting our partner as they are deepens the connection perhaps more than any single factor. When, after much ineffective effort, we accept the futility of trying to change our partner, there comes a great freedom, both for ourselves and for the other. Once we release the mental, emotional, and physical constriction associated with fruitless effort, a deep release and relaxation results at all these levels. When we take the pressure off our partner, they too experience release from constriction. We create the conditions under which our partner can find the interior space to accept us and make changes from within as a positive choice, rather than remaining stuck in a pattern of resisting our coercion.

The alternative to focusing on trying to change the other is, of course, acceptance of our partner as they are, focusing instead on *ourselves* as the locus of change. This approach is both kinder to our partner, which supports intimacy, and a far more empowering practice for ourselves. Owning our thoughts and feelings, then learning from them rather than making our inner experience the responsibility of the other, allows us to move progressively toward being who we want to be. Not trying to change another, allowing them to be as they are, is the strongest message of acceptance we can give. And, acceptance is love in action. It contributes far more to building intimacy in the long run than any sweet nothings you can whisper in your beloved's ear.

Conversely, when we are pushing to change our partner, we send a strong critical signal of judgment. "You are not okay the way you are. To be okay you need to be the way I want you to be." Such an attitude results in emotional distance. This does not mean that we shouldn't communicate to our partner what we want and need. It means we can express our thoughts and feelings with even greater ease because both partners know that the expression is without coercion and without attachment to outcome. Both understand it is an expression, not a demand. This is a critical difference.

The challenge is to express ourselves fully, but not to expect change from our partner as a result—not to be attached to "that which I want will be given." Rather, it is to accept "how it is," and to learn from what is happening within ourselves under the conditions of how it is. If fortune shines upon us and our partner gives us the gift of a change in their behavior, the skillful response is to accept it graciously and continue not to expect change the next time.

I saw this enacted on the beach the other day in the difference in attitude and behavior between two little girls as they played with a dog. The first girl was trying her hardest to force the dog, Elijah, to give up the ball so that she could play throw and retrieve with him. Elijah would not drop the ball for her. He sensed, as animals often do, the coercion, and so resisted it. This first little girl walked away frustrated and crying, unable to change Elijah's behavior. The second little girl, now alone with Elijah, simply waited quietly, speaking appreciations softly and gently to the dog. Elijah dropped the ball right in front of her and played throw and retrieve with her for a long time, accompanied by the sounds of the little girl's shouts of joy and pleasure.

Similarly, the many programs focused on alcohol abuse—institutions that work with people who most need to change—know this principle well. Al Anon, an organization that works with people who have an alcoholic in their families, strongly encourages its members not to try to change the alcoholic, even though it is clear the alcoholic needs to change. Most members have tried many times to manipulate, coerce, or cajole the alcoholic into stopping drinking, with no success, and at a great cost to themselves. The fundamental message of Al Anon is "do not try to change the other, change yourself." The message is to make the changes in your own life that support a happier, more satisfying existence. If that means leave, then leave; if that means stay, then stay. But do not waste your precious life trying to change another, no matter how much they need changing. It does not work, and is usually counterproductive.

The transformation of perspective from trying to change the other to acceptance of the other, along with the shift in the locus of change from you to me, is monumental and extremely challenging. It rises to the level of a paradigm shift, a movement from one deeply ingrained worldview and all the behaviors that emanate from it, to a new conceptual framework and new behavioral patterns. The change can also be described as a shift in emphasis from *action* to *inquiry*. The focus changes from an emphasis on behavior—"what should I do to get you to change?"—to self-examination. The accent is on asking, "what am *I* experiencing at all levels of my being?", which allows my actions to flow from that inquiry. The shift is thus toward noting my inner responses to what I am experiencing in the presence of the other at such depth that my actions, rather than being conditioned responses or strategically constructed behaviors, flow more easily and naturally out of the resulting insight and understanding.

An example of this process is the very challenging question many of us face at one time or another as to whether we should stay in a relationship or leave it. Generally, the way we do this is to agonize over what is the correct action, whether we should leave or stay. We drive ourselves crazy scouring our list of what is positive and negative in the relationship, trying to develop the cognitive answer so that we can take the "right" action. It works better to *sit with* the process, deeply experiencing the feelings we are undergoing without focusing on the action of whether to stay or leave. From this experience, insight and understanding will arise about our self, about our history and conditioning, and about what feels right at a gut level. This inner knowing will direct us toward what to *do*, producing an outcome in which we can have more confidence.

As we have seen, the movement of turning inward before acting outward has benefits that go beyond building intimacy. It also supports our own personal growth. One important way it does this is by serving as a healing antidote for our early loss of self, which has set us up for codependency in intimate relationship. As children, most of us were conditioned to turn outward for self-definition rather than find it within ourselves. We continue to do this as adults, especially in intimate relationship. This results in the tendency for our partner's state of mind and emotions to determine our own state of mind and emotions. We need them to be happy for us to be happy, and so on.

When we move toward staying in our own skin, not trying to change the other, we are forced back upon our self, taking responsibility for our own happiness. We learn to define who we are independently, based upon our own thoughts and feelings. We are then more separate from the moods of the other. We can be caring and compassionate towards our partner without needing them to be different. It actually builds intimacy to allow the other their sadness or pain rather than trying to talk them out of it so that we can feel better.

The expectation that the other needs to change, and that we can change them, creates a constriction within our bodies. It literally creates a physical tightening; if we pay attention, this easily can be felt as a physical sensation somewhere in the body. When we let go of expectations, there is a tendency towards release and a feeling of expansion, a relaxation and opening in the body. This information, which comes directly from the body, does not lie. The letting go of expectations and control is good for our overall wellbeing.

The gift we give our partner in doing this is allowing them the space to experience the joy of being who they are, as they are, without the negativity of coercion. Under these conditions we actually increase the possibility of "getting what we want" because when they are no longer frozen into reacting to our coercion, they can more easily give us that offering.

Gayle was in a relationship with a man she professed to love deeply, who shared values that were important to her. But, she tried so hard to change Barry that she drove him and herself half crazy. "He needs to be more demonstrative, affectionate, and committed," she said. These demands for "more" drove a deep wedge between her and Barry. He felt he was being authentic in his love for her, and committed to their relationship. He explained that in his family of origin, people were not demonstrative, so it didn't feel natural or comfortable for him to be so. But this explanation was not good enough for Gayle. She continued to try to change him through her insistence, until Barry finally couldn't take it any more and left the relationship. Gayle ended up heartbroken. Her efforts to change her partner resulted in exactly the opposite of what she wanted. If Gayle had stayed within her own skin and accepted the level of love and affection Barry was capable of giving, and had gone vertically within herself to better understand her own strong reactions to "not getting enough," she might not have ended up alone.

When we commit to not trying to change the other, we have to learn to deal with the disappointment of not getting what we want. Of course, we have that same disappointment when we do try to change the other, because it seldom works. However, the inner resources developed through the practice of focusing inward, minimizing expectations, and counting on ourselves for strength, makes it easier to withstand disappointment. The irony in this is that the narcissistic joke, "it's all about me," is at a deeper level actually true. When we are triggered by our partner's behavior, the skillful first assumption is to know deep down and act on the knowledge that "it really is all about me," even though our habitual tendency is to assume "it's all about you."

A happier story than Gayle and Barry's is that of Kelly and Mark. Kelly complained for years about not having satisfying sex with her husband. He wasn't sensitive enough and didn't touch her as she wanted. Mark was confused and frustrated by this. He felt he listened carefully to everything his wife asked for, and was trying his best to meet her needs. After working with the concepts of "staying in our own skin" and "not trying to change the other," Kelly finally got it. She started taking responsibility for her own orgasm. Interestingly, she soon started finding that her sexual life with Mark was much improved. "I'm owning it now," she said. "I am, for the first time in my life, allowing myself to open to sexual pleasure. It is so clear to me at this point that both the good sex and the bad sex are my responsibility. If I hadn't stopped trying to change Mark and really looked at myself, I think we would both have continued to be frustrated and grown more distant."

Anthony had a similar experience around jealousy. He blamed and harped on his girlfriend Rita to the point of almost breaking up their relationship. Because, he said, "I know you put on that perfume to attract Richard," their mutual friend. No matter what Rita said to deny her interest in Richard, and despite the lack of any real behavior indicating an attraction, Anthony would not be swayed. After much conflict and pain, Anthony came to see that the real issue was not Rita or Richard, but his own chronic jealousy. This stemmed, of course, from his personal history. Anthony was able to say to Rita, "What I now know is that when I smell that scent, this feeling I've known since I was a child comes over me. I don't understand its source yet, but when it happens again, instead of nagging, I am going to try to work on that stuff. I want to find a way to either let it go or deal with it, but not make it a relationship-breaker between us."

Owning our reactions is an act of peace. An act of nonviolence. At the core of nonviolence philosophy is the belief that peace starts within. It starts small and grows. If there is peace within us and within our relationships, then we are the best kind of activists for peace. As the Indian sage Patanjali, known as the "Father of Yoga," wrote, "When we are firmly established in nonviolence, beings around us cease feeling hostility."

The "blame and change" habit is the opposite of peacemaking. It is inherently violent, and tends to set off a cycle of blame and defense by encouraging the equal and opposite behavior in the other. It triggers the worst, not the best, in people. There seems to be an inherent desire within all of us to be "seen." To feel received for who we are, exactly as we are. If others accept us, it helps us accept ourselves. The act of not trying to change our partner is a wonderful way to love them, to support them in being seen, and to allow them to feel better about themselves. Being in intimate relationship with someone who feels good about who they are is a blessing. The "not trying to change the other" approach is one of the most loving things we can do to support our partner, and to help ourselves grow up.

6 ❧ Relationship to Our Self

An unexamined life is not worth living.
SOCRATES

To be truly intimate with another requires that we first be intimate with ourselves. Getting closer to ourselves by engaging in an ongoing process of self-inquiry and self-understanding makes it possible to have a deeper connection with our partner.

A wonderful metaphor for the primacy of working on oneself in order to be available for one's partner is the announcement we hear before airplane takeoff: "If you are traveling with a companion, secure your own mask before helping others." If we lack the insight that results from an examined life, all kinds of unconscious and destructive behavior will leak into our relationships. However, if we are engaged in the ongoing process of working to understand ourselves, thereby reducing our limiting habitual patterns, we can better avoid the automatic behaviors that are harmful, and choose instead actions that support intimacy.

Some years ago, I was working with a group of high-powered corporate executives who earned a trip to a seminar I was giving on Life Balance. Most complained that they could not find an appropriate equilibrium between their commitment to work and their commitment to family. Things always seemed to be out of balance in one direction or another. Either they felt they were devoting too much time to work and too little to family, or vice versa. With considerable discussion and some deep self-reflection, the consensus that emerged was that the source of the imbalance, of the problems in their relationship to work and family, was at bottom a poor relationship to themselves. Though bright, energetic, and highly successful in the material realm, they were giving short shrift to their inner experience. True deep, reflective self-inquiry was not a part of their regular activity. They were not intimate with themselves, and therefore not in satisfactory relationship to work and family.

The graphic we developed to illustrate this was a teeter-totter, with work and family on the seats, and self as the triangular foundation centered underneath. The self is the foundation upon which all the other elements rest. The obvious conclusion to us all was that it is mandatory for that base of self to be well-tended and sound in order for the life elements that rest upon it to work properly.

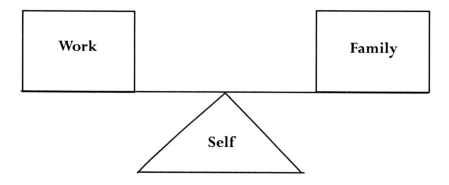

To be intimate with ourselves means getting close to who we really are, understanding what is actually occurring moment to moment within us. Not necessarily understanding ourselves in a static way or in some grand philosophical sense, but as an embrace of our actual inner experience. It means being real with ourselves about how we are experiencing the world we live in, and honoring our human tendency toward denial and delusion even as we struggle to open to our interior encounter as it unfolds. It means being aware that we are angry when we are experiencing anger, sad when we are experiencing sadness. It means being aware that we are thinking negative thoughts when we are, or feeling blue or joyful, and not denying it to ourselves because it does not fit our preferred self-image. To be unaware or in denial of our inner experience is to be vulnerable to a pattern of habitual conditioned responses: unchosen reflexive behavior that is unskillful and often damaging to relationship.

A common and destructive form of this non-awareness is unconsciously treating our partner as if they were someone other than who they really are, someone else in our personal history. This involves transferring reactions to our beloved that are really to other important figures in our life without knowing that we are doing so. This process of transferring and projecting is normal and common in intimate relationships. Something in our partner's words or behaviors triggers a deep-seated reaction from our personal history, then without knowing it, we treat them as if they were that original historical figure. The antidote to this harmful pattern is self-awareness, looking closely at our inner experience and understanding what is truly going on so that we can make a choice rather than emit a reaction. This may involve noting, for example, that our anger in the moment may not be a true response to our wife's behavior in the present, but a reaction to our mother's dominance many years ago. Without vigorous moment-to-moment self-inquiry, these types of destructive processes can dominate our relationships and destroy intimacy.

I am guilty of this very phenomenon. Because I had a strong mother and was a rebellious child, I am overly sensitive to control. When Barbara offers some information in the spirit of simply trying to be helpful or supportive, with no intent to control, unless my self-awareness is keenly tuned in I am capable of experiencing it as control, and unconsciously lashing out as a defensive reaction. This behavior is not really in response to her, but a conditioned reaction deriving from my personal history.

An essential aspect of intimacy is mutual understanding. Communication is a key ingredient enabling this understanding. Sharing our interior self with our partner—those aspects about which we feel vulnerable and which we tend to guard—is a great gift of trust, and very much deepens the relationship. This kind of self-revealing, so essential to intimacy, is impossible without self-awareness. If we are not in touch with our own real thoughts and feelings, we cannot share them. Under these conditions what we are left with, at best, is sharing the same illusions and delusions we have about ourselves with our partner. Illusion and delusion do not foster intimacy. Self-awareness through self-examination is not optional if we are truly to have a close connection with our partner.

To be intimate with oneself is a call for authenticity. For being real. As real with oneself as possible, so we can be real with another. If we remain in the mask, behind a façade, then whom are we offering to our partner? Only a ghost. And how can we be intimate with a ghost? There are many façades we humans use to avoid our authenticity: playing strong, weak, cool, smart, stupid, and many other strategies to get by without really making ourselves known to ourselves or our partner. We developed these masks in childhood to survive the challenges of our youth. Now, however, as adults, these façades no longer serve us. In fact they inhibit authenticity and the possibility of intimacy.

A common pose is the façade of "being nice." Not being kind, which is authentic, openhearted giving, but *nice*, which is a fabricated manner for getting by in the world without upsetting others. To maintain this façade we must deny our true inner experience. We replace anger with nice, sadness with nice, frustration with nice, and so on.

Authenticity implies honesty—honesty first with our self, and then with the other. Honesty in the sense that we see and acknowledge what is really going on within us, not just what we want to be going on. Communicating from a place of honesty about our inner experience builds intimacy because it opens us up to our partner and lets them into who we are. If we can find the courage to share with this sort of integrity, our relationship can flourish.

If we are angry, it is important to be aware that we are in a state of anger so that our actions under these conditions can be skillful and by choice rather than reactive and destructive. The person who is in the habit of maintaining the façade may have no awareness that they are angry, or sad, or whatever "not nice" emotion they are having. They are in danger of losing the mask and, in their lack of awareness, lashing out with damaging words or behavior.

One man we worked with, whose wife was having an affair, walked away from the relationship then later returned. He said to us, "if I was in touch with myself, I would have been more in touch with her and this would never have happened. It was my lack of being there, being present, being aware. My lack of being me produced all this. It's a lesson I won't forget."

Beyond the moment-to-moment awareness of our experience, it is difficult to define what constitutes the structure of the self that we wish to understand. What constitutes the *me* into which I am inquiring? This is a philosophical question that has no firm or right answer. One useful way to look at the structure of self, however, is to use the Jungian model, which views the person as having four components: the physical, mental, emotional, and spiritual.

Awareness of the physical self, being mindful of what our body is experiencing, is a key to our health and our ability to sustain a satisfying, productive life. It is the mental, emotional, and spiritual elements of our self, however, that must be better understood to foster intimacy.

Our mental aspect holds the key to our *Core Beliefs*, the deep-seated ideas about our self and the world in which we live, which organize our experience and in so doing largely create our destiny. Our Core Beliefs, which are often not conscious, but hidden under layers of denial and illusion, are best acknowledged, thoroughly examined, and understood in order to appreciate what organizing principles govern our behavior. Through a deeper understanding of our Core Beliefs, the organizing conceptual principles that are the sources of behavior, we can come closer to being their master rather than their servant.

We have worked with many people who are not in intimate relationship, have not been for a long time, and are extremely frustrated because they desire relationship intensely. What we have learned about this phenomenon is that there is often an even stronger set of unseen beliefs beneath the longing to be in relationship that actually directs their behavior towards avoiding relationship rather than creating it. Upon examining their Core Beliefs, some of these people find that, for reasons embedded in their personal history, they actually believe it is dangerous to be in an intimate relationship. Or that they do not deserve to be in a relationship, or that the opposite sex is inferior, or some equivalent relationship-rejecting belief. When unexamined and not understood, these deep mental constructs can inhibit the possibility of getting what we

desire. Perhaps even worse, having these inhibiting beliefs but still finding our way into relationship keeps us from ever being intimate with our
partner.

The emotional element is perhaps the most important component of
the self that needs ongoing examination in order to understand what we
truly feel beneath the fantasy of what we want ourselves to feel, or think
we should feel. In order to gain some freedom from its often limiting
nature, or to make skillful choices of behavior, we need to know what is
emotionally so. This I call *Emotional Wisdom* work.

If we feel frustration on the job, for instance, and come home grumpy
and unsettled, it is important to know what we are actually feeling, and
perhaps have some insight into its source. Too often, however, what happens under these conditions is that some aspect of our partner's quite
innocent speech or behavior triggers the unconscious emotion, and
the underlying frustration jumps out as hostility. We have thus created
unnecessary separation from, and resentment in, our beloved. Alternatively, if we know our frustration for what it is, we can share how we feel
and thus build greater intimacy through communication.

To deepen the connection with another, it is of great benefit to connect with our own individual sense of spirituality. For me it is important
to remember in the hubbub of daily life that there is a part of me that is
unconditioned, quiet, and calm: a higher part of me than my personality, a part that resides deep within, naturally dwelling in harmony and
peace. The essential quality of this quiet core self is love. I find it important to devote time to nourishing this *Spiritual Core*. When I identify with
it I am kinder to myself and I make better decisions about my behavior
toward others. It also allows me to be more open and accepting of my
partner. We cannot fully love another until we love our self. Because the
true nature of our Spiritual Core is love, being in touch with that center,
the part that fully accepts and does not judge, supports an intimate, loving relationship.

It is so important that our partner feel accepted and appreciated by
us. Judgment is an intimacy-breaker. To be in touch with that nonjudg-
mental and accepting spiritual part of ourselves is a great gift to our

relationship. To be appreciative and accepting often requires that we at least temporarily drop our own limitations and hurts in order to be there for the other. This involves a high level of self-development. To live at this level we need to be masters rather than servants of our thoughts and feelings, and to be able to access our Spiritual Core. When we work with couples we call this *Dropping the Bag*.

As I discuss more fully below, each of us has a "bag" full of our own bruises, wounds, and limitations that get triggered by the other. Often the same issue triggers both people in the relationship. It is as if certain matters become a two-sided sword. Each side cuts one of the partners in a different way, yet hurts both. Unless one partner can find the awareness and skill to drop their bag of woes and listen in sympathetic presence while the other explores their triggered place, the moment turns into a highly charged, often destructive interaction.

We worked with a couple just the other day: the man felt very sensitive to blame, and his wife felt chronically misunderstood. So when Marcia felt misunderstood and expressed her frustration at not being listened to, Ben felt blamed. When this happened, he became agitated, and angrily blamed her in return. As a result, Marcia felt further misunderstood, and the negative cycle drove deeper holes in their connection.

To do the difficult work of turning this kind of cycle in a more positive direction, one person must, through the process of ongoing self-inquiry, be developed enough to become aware that they have been triggered. They must choose not to react in a habitual manner, and instead be a neutral healing presence for the other. In this case, if Ben can learn to be aware of his chronic reaction to what he perceives as criticism, he has the possibility of dropping his bag, putting it aside at least temporarily, and listening. Then Marcia is likely to feel understood and complete. It becomes possible for Marcia to be at ease enough to drop her bag and support Ben in working on healing his sensitivity to blame.

In becoming intimate with oneself, one can begin to conquer the debilitating effects of codependency. As I have said, codependency is fundamentally a state of being in which we are sufficiently out of touch with our self that we unconsciously try to live through our partner's experience.

This condition makes life very difficult for both us and our partner when it reaches the point where we need the other to be happy in order to be happy our self. The antidote to codependency is being in touch with our self. We must first be separate before we can give our self to another. We cannot give our self if there is no true independent self to give. When we find that we are out of touch with our self, and that we need to make our partner feel differently so that we can feel better, it is time to make a change. It is time to bring our attention to our self. How are we experiencing our self? How are we feeling? What are we thinking?

Unfortunately, it is rare in relationship for partners to take full responsibility for their own happiness, and not to unconsciously give that responsibility over to the other. The opposite is also true. It is rare for most of us not to take responsibility for the other's happiness and allow that work to remain theirs. A Sufi saying highlights the paradox of this common pattern: "Within your own house dwells the treasure of joy, so why do you go begging from door to door?"

The practical application of this perspective is called *Methodological Individualism*. It is an approach to improving relationship that focuses on the individuals more than on the entity called "the relationship." The people in the relationship are the living, breathing flesh-and-blood entities that can be touched, affected, changed. The entity called the relationship has no body, blood, or guts. It is a concept, a process, a structure, an energetic pattern within which the partners function. It can't change without the individuals in it making an alteration. The healing in the Healing Relationship is that of the individuals in the context of the relationship. Our partner triggers our sleeping wounds, which, by being brought forth, can be healed. And in healing we each make our self more available to our partner.

It all comes down to awareness and choice. An examined life is a life of self-awareness: awareness of who we are in both a larger sense, and in the more microscopic, moment-to-moment unfolding of our thoughts and feelings. With awareness, choice then becomes possible. When we see our options, we can choose patterns that support intimacy rather than those that destroy it.

7 ❧ Core Beliefs

We see what we believe.

A complex system of *Core Beliefs,* which often lies below the level of conscious access, informs many of our attitudes and guides our behavior. Core Beliefs are deeply ingrained ideas—often old, unexamined, and frequently having their origins in childhood—that guide much of our behavior in the present. What we believe significantly shapes the reality we create and live in. Consciously or unconsciously, our Core Beliefs direct our perceptions, attitudes, and behavioral responses to the people and things in our environment. To a large extent our Core Beliefs also determine the responses of the environment to us. In this circular way our Core Beliefs sculpt our lives.

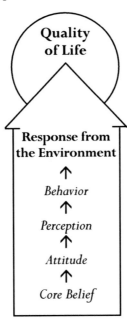

It is important, therefore, to examine our belief system to understand to what degree it supports our desire for intimacy, or conversely, serves as a force to defeat it. Becoming aware of the Core Beliefs that organize our attitudes, perceptions, and behavior around relationship, then shifting them into belief patterns that support intimacy, is one of the most elegant and powerful ways to improve our lives.

For example, my life may seem full of personal failure and victimization, causing me confusion, suffering, and anger at the world around me. Underneath, at the level of cause, deeper than I have access to or consciously know, it may be that my life experiences have conditioned me to believe that "I am not good enough." This Core Belief has a profound effect on my attitudes, perceptions, and behavior. If I were to become aware of that deep organizing belief and shift it towards "I am good enough just the way I am," a very different flow of attitudes, perceptions, and behavioral responses to the world around me would emerge. I am no longer a "failure," no longer a "victim," and the reality of my life will increasingly mimic these views.

These deep-seated belief patterns usually originate in, and are conditioned by, our cultural, social, and personal psychological history. They drive us and shape our lives. For example, the belief "I can't sing," or "I can't dance," or "paint," or etc., often arises from an early message we received from parents or teachers that "you are not artistic." We later introject, or take as our own, those externally generated beliefs. They become part of our core organizing conceptual system.

Similarly, but far more troubling and antithetical to intimacy, is the belief engendered by a punitive environment that people are dangerous and the world is inherently unsafe. The obvious result in behavior is to avoid relationship, or if we are in one, to remain distant enough to keep ourselves protected. If I become aware of this Core Belief and choose to shift it towards, for example, the belief that "people are safe until they prove themselves unsafe," then my attitudes, perceptions and behavior will shift in thousands of microscopic ways to align with that belief, and in most cases produce a reality on the screen of my life that reflects it. Imagine the difference in one's experience of life if the organizing attitude is "life is a struggle" versus "life flows like the river."

Money is often a source of conflict in relationship. Core Beliefs around money are very powerful, and significantly affect both our material status in the world and the quality of our relationship. Those fortunate enough to have been conditioned to believe that "there is enough," in contrast to those who have been conditioned to believe the opposite, have a very different experience in life. The former tend to be more at peace with themselves about money, and at ease with their partners around material concerns. The latter tend to worry and struggle within themselves, and also find money to be a major source of friction with their partners.

Examining our Core Beliefs is not about judging our self as right or wrong. It is about discovering the foundation or mental architecture upon which our life experience is built. This enables us to choose a belief system that is authentic and congruent with who we want to be. Core Beliefs about the nature of relationship vary widely, and profoundly affect whether or not we are in relationship, the quality of relationship, and the depth of our intimacy.

A common destructive Core Belief that causes a great deal of frustration is "finding a partner will make me happy." Amongst people who are not in relationship, this generates a desperation that is terribly uncomfortable, and creates an air of neediness that is off-putting to potential partners, who feel the neediness and run in the opposite direction. This creates even greater desperation, and worsens the chances for a satisfactory outcome in the future.

This phenomenon, like most of the principles discussed in this book, is not specific either to gender or sexual orientation. A gay man in one of our relationship workshops was so consumed by his longing for a partner that he turned off every potential partner in his proximity. He found himself not only without an intimate partner, but also isolated from the entire workshop community. A woman in that same workshop, Doris, expressed a common complaint: "I want to be in a relationship, but I never seem to be in one that lasts." Upon reflection, a previously unrecognized belief emerged that at a deeper level, Doris believed that relationships inevitably result in "restriction" and "the end of personal freedom." She discovered a behavioral pattern in which every time she got close to someone, a sense of discomfort emerging from this belief arose. Ultimately, Doris always found a way to be rejected by the other. Thus, she unskillfully accomplished the goal of her Core Belief. She was unhappily "free from restriction." So while Doris, like many people, longed for an intimate relationship, there existed within her a stronger unconscious Core Belief working in the opposite direction. Though she was unaware of it, it guided her behavior in a direction that conflicted with what she more consciously desired.

Similarly, Heather longed for intimate relationship and continued to find it only in married and otherwise unavailable men. When she examined her belief structure, some surprising material emerged. By dropping into her feelings through a process I discuss more fully later, Heather learned some key things about herself that limited her ability to have what she wanted. Most importantly, Heather realized the defining impact on her of her father's belief system and the way he interacted with her. When she delved into feelings that she came to associate with her father, the phrase emerged "in order to be with you, I have to give up me." This Heather understood as having originated in her father's inability to accept her as she was, and his ability to love her only when she thought and acted in ways he approved. Consequently, while at the conscious level Heather wanted to be in relationship with a man, something deeper told her she would have to abandon herself to do it. At that deep level she was not willing to sacrifice herself for a relationship. As a result, Heather had remained single, unaware as to why, and frustrated. Knowing this, Heather now has a choice. She can continue acting upon this belief inherited from her father, or release that constricting belief and choose to enter freely into a relationship.

A destructive Core Belief that many in our society carry is "I am not worthy, I am not lovable." Consequently, when we are given love there is a tendency to reject it, because at some deeper level we feel we do not deserve it. A sad outcome of this syndrome happened in the case of a man I came to know in an organizational context, who ultimately became so depressed that he took his own life. Some months before he had said to me, "It is hard for me to receive love and support because most of my life I haven't gotten it. When I do, I have a hard time feeling I deserve it."

Similarly, a culturally accepted, yet ultimately destructive, Core Belief is that intimate relationship is driven by romantic love and lusty sexuality. Its corollary is that romance and sexual passion inevitably fade over time. This fallacious principle is parodied in the media by television sitcoms that mock long-term committed relationship by featuring the controlling wife and the overly compliant husband, or the boring relationship with the passive wife and the overly aggressive husband. Rather than framing the challenges of long-term relationship as opportunities to grow, these images of unsatisfying relationships lead people to accept as "normal" a sense of the inevitable failure of intimacy. There are many more such limiting Core Beliefs that, if not examined, will cause us to miss the life we deserve.

Paradigm Shifting

If we accept that Core Beliefs significantly influence the quality of our lives, then it is important to understand the concept of paradigm and paradigm shifting. A paradigm is a conceptual pattern, a structured set of beliefs, that defines and describes for us the nature of the world within and without. A paradigm is essentially a complex of Core Beliefs that, taken together, form a worldview. Paradigms constitute the elements of our conceptual architecture.

Our personal paradigms, because they are an amalgam of Core Beliefs, control and affect us in an even deeper way than any single Core Belief. Shifting our internal paradigms is an elegant and powerful force for transformation. We enable ourselves to move from one universe to another. The world we experience transforms with just a rearrangement of pathways in the brain. Demonstrating the elegance and simplicity of this was a statement by the Indian Teacher Ramana Maharshi. When asked why he doesn't travel, he replied, "Why bother? I can go there in my mind."

One important and powerful paradigm shift that supports the development of intimacy is the previously mentioned shift in priority from action to inquiry. As Westerners, we are conditioned to value action.

The person of action is highly esteemed. Cultural heroes are often action figures like the American icons John Wayne or Bruce Willis. The cultural paradigm here may be stated as "action is primary." We constantly hear statements like, "Well that's fine, but what are you going to do about it?" Inquiry holds a place lower in the pecking order than action.

This is clearly antithetical to the principle that self-inquiry is a prerequisite to satisfactory and intimate relationship. In the interest of intimacy, I propose that we shift our internal paradigm to one that values inquiry over action. This means a change in the direction of honoring the internal process as primary, and seeing the external action as a natural out-flowing from this inquiry. Action should be seen as secondary, an outcome of the process of self-investigation. Action naturally flows from considered inquiry. When action alone is emphasized, it seldom comes from a sufficiently deep or considered place to yield a satisfactory result. When we take life's challenges as an opportunity to look within ourselves, then let the action flow easily from that place, more skillful behavior emerges. The key question shifts from "What should I do?" to "What am I experiencing?"

For example, we may be asking ourselves, "Should I stay in relationship with this person or should I leave it?" Wrong question! This focus puts primary emphasis on the action and trying to figure out which activity will produce the best outcome. The superior alternative is to focus on the inquiry, on fully feeling the tension within ourselves as we experience these two alternatives. This moves our attention and energy towards becoming aware of what is being triggered inside of us by this relationship: How are we feeling? What's happening in our body? What insights arise when we allow ourselves to experience this dilemma fully? This diminishes the emphasis on deciding to launch into action, and instead brings our awareness and focus to the inner encounter. If we focus our attention in this way, the most skillful and integrated action tends to emerge naturally out of the state of equilibrium created when the inner process reaches completion. The accent here is not so much on problem-solving as it is on examining the fullness of the problem, mining it for what we can learn emotionally, conceptually, and spiritually. The problem becomes our teacher, and we its student.

Right action flows out of this paradigm. It is our mistrust of self and our self-critical nature that most undermine our confidence to act naturally and wisely, forcing an obsession with action. One of the major weaknesses of our primary emphasis on action is that it rushes us into left-brain analytical function alone. It inevitably produces some form of list-making, the positives on one side, the negatives on the other. Though this approach makes logical sense, it is seldom truly satisfying. It is inadequate because it is partial and not integrated. It focuses only on the analytical, and leaves out the emotional and spiritual components of our reality. When we emphasize inquiry, we engage both sides of the brain: the analytical function of the left hemisphere, and the intuitive, creative wisdom of the right. Thus we go beyond the lists to integrate other ways of knowing, those of the gut and the heart. From this fuller knowing, more satisfying action flows for ourselves, for our partners, and for our relationship.

When we shift the emphasis toward attention to the internal process, we become aware of the feelings: the joy, sadness, fear, hope, and doubt that arise in experiencing the challenges life provides us. When shared, these are exactly the components that make up and strengthen intimate connection. When the conventional paradigm is accepted, the tendency is to deny feelings, defining them as impediments to action. In denying the fear and doubt, the joy and hope, in not allowing the feelings to carry their messages, we miss valuable information that teaches us about our self, about our healthy and wounded places, and about what action is truly skillful.

In this alternative paradigm we are also moving from an emphasis on the noun, representing complete fixed outcomes, to the verb, representing deeds and beings in process. As already noted, moving from an accent on relationship to an emphasis on relating allows us to treat our interpersonal connections as a constant unfolding. It is a learning process, where we are constantly growing our understanding of what works and what doesn't, what feels good and what doesn't, what strengthens connection and what weakens it. We open the possibility to make adjustments based upon the unfolding lessons. When we focus on relationship—the noun, a completed structure—we must either accept or reject it. As a verb, it is in a constant state of motion, a constant state of becoming.

An interesting example showing the depth and power of Core Beliefs and paradigms in shaping the quality of our existence involves that larger-than-life American institution, the Super Bowl. Many years after the Minnesota Vikings lost a Super Bowl game, their on-field captain and quarterback, Fran Tarkington, said, "There isn't a day that goes by that I don't have pain about that loss—what could I have done differently? We damaged the state of Minnesota." How painful, on an ongoing basis, this one event was for a very successful man, both on and off the field, because of his fixed belief around the importance of winning. The coach of that same Minnesota Vikings team, Bud Grant, while being interviewed about the game said, "Life is no different for me, win or lose. We would still be sitting here enjoying the sunshine." Given exactly the same objective circumstances and outcome, Bud's life continued to be joyful and fulfilled, while Fran's carried a despondency long after the event. The only difference between the two was the subtle and invisible Core Beliefs driving their experience of Life.

8 ✣ Emotional Wisdom

...and the time came when the risk it took to remain in a tightly closed
bud became infinitely more painful than the risk it took to blossom.
ANAÏS NIN

Emotional Wisdom work is the process of turning our challenging feelings into insight and liberation. Emotional Wisdom is like
the philosopher's stone. It can turn lead into gold, change our inner discomfort into personal freedom, and serve as an important ally in finding, developing, and supporting relationship. Despite our widespread
reluctance to allow and deeply experience our feelings, doing so is a
doorway to liberation, and an opening to intimacy. While our hardwir-
ing and habits tend toward embracing pleasure and pushing away pain,
there is much to be gained by choosing inquiry into both kinds of feelings. To truly experience the sensations that accompany our emotions,
whether pleasant or unpleasant, is a learned skill. It is almost always the
case that if we slow down and focus our attention on the bodily feelings
that accompany our emotional states, important information about the
sources of our reactivity and constriction is revealed.

The process of attending to these sensations tends incrementally or
dramatically to clear and release unconscious blocks and conditioned
responses associated with previous emotional wounding, producing great
benefits. We become more capable of choosing our actions, rather than
slavishly reacting to whatever stimuli appear in our environment. We
are empowered to choose actions that support intimacy instead of those
that damage it. Over time, we can become clear enough to identify and
consequently reject, believe, or react to our partner's unskillful actions
emanating from their reactivity. Because the source of our chronic reactivity has been reduced or eliminated, our partner's contrary behavior

has nowhere to stick on us. We can be with them in a supportive way instead of succumbing to a negative cycle of conflict.

The more we find the courage to feel deeply and stay with the feelings until release occurs and/or insights emerge, the better able we are to contact and understand the source of our restrictions and reactivity. As we approach this causal level, the ability to heal the original wounding becomes possible. Because it is so spot-on, it has become cliché to understand our emotional problems as having their source in hurtful childhood experiences. It is still true, however, that our culture's child-rearing practices have remained largely in the dark ages, and continue to produce considerable emotional wounding to our children. Though some of us have had what we would call a "happy childhood," many of us have not. And no matter how "happy" we think our childhood was, there are inevitably points in our formative history that were emotionally hurtful, whether the wounding involved parents, other adults, or peers. Childhood wounds go deep because our slate is so clean and our defenses so undeveloped at that point in our lives. As stated in its worst form by Lloyd de Mause, "The history of childhood is a nightmare from which we have only begun to awaken."

Karen's story about her chronic difficulties with intimate relationships illustrates the value of dropping into the emotional body to discover the root cause of the surface symptoms. In a workshop with us, Karen recounted her continuing frustration with not finding or being able to sustain a satisfying relationship with a man. When I guided her into fully feeling this sense of frustration, an image emerged for her of a heart. A human heart. As she stayed with that image, she noticed it was a "hardened heart that feels closed and imprisoned." I asked her to dialog with that image, asking it, "What do you need?" The imaginary heart, a manifestation and conduit for the wisdom of the unconscious mind, simply said, "Love." Then an image arose of her father, and a remembrance of him as a "big man with a big heart who got stomped on by my mother." With those words came a deep feeling of sadness and a torrent of tears. I asked Karen to slow down even further and really let in the feelings she was experiencing. "My heart is softening," she said, "and I can see it opening." A few months later I saw Karen again. She told me she was in a satisfying relationship with a man named Peter, and that they both were committed to making it a long-term bond.

Emotional Wisdom work of this type provides an opportunity to gain freedom from negative patterns, bit by bit, over a lifetime. We can move toward a return to the expansiveness and freedom of our original state, before the emotional wounding. A quote from *A Course in Miracles* expresses this well: "Your task is not to seek for love, but merely to seek and find all of the barriers within yourself that you have built against it."

Staying only with the cognitive and conceptual aspect of inquiry does not allow for the Emotional Wisdom approach to unfold. The knowledge from the analytical channel is useful, but only partial. When we are engaged in conceptual analysis, we are working with information that is conscious and already available to us. We have mined it thoroughly already, many times over. So if the feelings are still there, it is not likely to be solved by digging in the same unproductive mine.

My client Sara was still suffering terribly three years after the breakup of a relationship that had lasted three years. She was forever torturing herself with the mental questions, "Why did he leave me? Why did we break up? What is wrong with me?" At that cognitive level of inquiry, she could never find an answer. She continued to go round and round in a futile effort at analysis, coming up frustrated and empty while driving herself deeper into unhappiness. For Sara, this kind of inquiry, limited to the analytical plane, was a diversion from fully feeling the grief of her loss. The ugly paradox here is that the effort to avoid feeling the pain by remaining on the mental channel prolonged her suffering. When Sara finally surrendered to truly experiencing the discomfort of her loss, the pain at first intensified and then rather quickly began to subside. Gradually, after a few months, Sara was finally ready to move forward in her life.

A wonderful technique for increasing Emotional Wisdom was developed by the psychiatrist Eugene Gendlin. Called *focusing*, it is a powerful tool for converting feelings into self-awareness, for fully feeling our feelings and extracting from them the insight that can free us from the reactivity that damages intimacy.[2] An aspect of this approach is clearly differentiating emotions from feelings. *Feelings* can be understood as physical sensations we experience in our body. *Emotions* can be understood as the sum of these physical feelings, plus the thoughts that accompany them. For example, the emotion of anger might be something like the complex of feeling hot, tight in the jaw, and constricted in the hands, accompanied by destructive, negative thoughts.

The technique of focusing uses the physical sensations in the body as the doorway to insight and release. The magic and mystery of it is that the body somehow acts as a conduit for bringing to consciousness the not-yet-conscious information that can be helpful in healing the sensitive places that are triggered when we experience an emotional wound. My particular version of this Emotional Wisdom technique can be outlined in the following way:

1. Take a comfortable position. To whatever extent possible, get into a relaxed and centered state of mind.

2. Bring up the emotion that is uncomfortable, then scan your body for the physical feelings that are associated with it.

3. Focus your attention on the part of your body that feels the most sensation. Gendlin refers to this as the "felt sense."

4. Go slowly. Be patient and drop deeply into the feeling without analyzing it. Just feel it fully and deeply.

5. Allow the feeling itself, not the conceptual process, to bubble up into your consciousness with a word or phrase that describes the fundamental quality of that feeling.

6. Beginning with the quality of that feeling, start a dialog with the physical part that is experiencing the felt sense in order to gain more insight into what is arising and what you are learning.

7. Some useful questions for the dialog are:

> Can you tell me more about this feeling?
> What does this part/feeling really want?
> What does this part/feeling really need?

8. If an image in your mind's eye arises and feels like a more dominant energy than the felt sense, use that image as a resource for wisdom, and dialog with it for information.

9. Encourage as much dialog as feels right with the images that emerge, or the place in the body where you feel the most sensation.

10. Stay with the process until you feel a sense of completion.

When we allow ourselves to drop deeply into the emotional body, observe closely whatever arises, dialog with images and the body, and allow insight to arise, both physical and emotional release tend to happen. Sometimes it is dramatic, sometimes incremental. All of it leads towards independence from reactivity, and expansion into free choice.

One can even disregard technique altogether and simply surrender to feeling one's feelings fully, then noticing the insight and release that spontaneously happen. What often occurs is that from the valley of discomfort and constriction, we rise to the peaks of joy and spaciousness. There seems to be a causal relationship between these two experiences and states of being. I have seen it and experienced it over and over again. When we really allow the anger, the grief, or the fear to run its course, we are left with the unexpected gift of elation. We are free from the uncomfortable aspect of the feelings and ready to experience the present unencumbered by the past.

This truth was hammered home to me by a group we were leading, when the participants complained to us that we were not going "deep enough" in our facilitation. I turned their projection around and asked the group, "What is stopping you from going deeper within yourselves?" They were taken aback. There was a brief silence, some moments of shuffling, and a bit of guttural noise. People began to inquire within themselves, understanding and then admitting that they were afraid of what might emerge from depth work. They avoided feeling deeply and talking about their experiences, using the excuse that they were stopping because they were taking up too much group time, or that they were boring the group with their story. They put themselves down or minimized their experience as a way of avoiding feeling into their true state. Once a substantial proportion of the group became conscious of this pattern in themselves, the mood of the individuals and the group was transformed. The atmosphere in the group became deeper, and many went on to find a measure of Emotional Wisdom in the work we did on ourselves that night.

There are numerous ways to access the wisdom hidden in the emotional body. Artistic expression is one of the best. Most creative processes call upon the emotional channel, and bring insight or burn off stuck energy, which allows for more productive thought and behavior. My wife and work partner, Barbara, is a gifted facilitator of creative expression. She specializes in using collage as a healing medium. Barbara provides a wide variety of visually and conceptually interesting materials, then asks people to choose images that naturally appeal to them and arrange them in a collage. When people complete the process, Barbara asks them to engage in a written dialog with the piece they have just created by using the dominant hand as the voice of the conscious mind that asks the questions, and the non-dominant hand as the conduit of not-yet-conscious material for the responses.

The information is sometimes surprising, and often provides important insights. Much Emotional Wisdom has emerged, and a lot of healing facilitated by this process. Barbara herself found release from an old emotional wound that came out of a brief, but terrifying incident of kidnapping when she was a young girl. She was abducted by a pedophile at the age of eleven, but quickly found a way to get out of his car. The experience, of course, was traumatic, and for a year afterwards she was in a chronic state of anxiety. Barbara traces a number of present-day sensitivities to that incident. One day, while doing a collage, she noticed that she had put the face of an ugly, aggressive looking man hidden in a paper pocket on the collage. In processing the work, she suddenly realized that it symbolized the pedophile. With that insight, a sense of release emerged that has allowed her to feel more emotionally whole in the present.

There are many other ways besides creative expression to access feelings and learn through them. Use whatever way suits you, because the process will promote self-healing and thereby support intimacy in your relationship.

9 ❦ The Wisdom Is in the Wound

Without your wounds where would your power be? The very angels themselves cannot persuade the wretched and blundering children on earth as can one human being broken in the wheels of living. In love's service, only the wounded soldier can serve.

THORNTON WILDER

Maturity, which is so important in sustaining a high quality intimate relationship, is largely the result of Emotional Wisdom. Getting more familiar with and understanding the four fundamental emotional states that dominate our emotional experience is helpful in supporting emotional maturity. The four states are *mad, sad, glad,* and *afraid.*

Anger, with its red heat, is a challenging emotional state. When we are in its grip, it is difficult to act wisely. Anger is so uncomfortable that it is hard to stay with the sensations it creates without externalizing it. Anger tends to demand release. When not consciously processed, the release can become verbally or physically violent. To deny feelings of anger, or in modern parlance to "stuff" them, is dangerous to ourselves. It causes frustration, high levels of internal distress, and can actually result in physical illness. Even when denied, anger tends to seep out at some later time in reactive and dysfunctional ways in response to petty and irrelevant behaviors from the people closest to us.

To neither lash out nor deny it, but to feel it fully, is the skillful way to experience anger. If we feel it completely, anger—like most emotions—will peak and then diminish in a wavelike manner. It begins, rises, crests to its zenith, then subsides and dissolves. Staying with the wave to its conclusion allows us to partially or fully release and be free of that particular anger. If we are fortunate, we may even gain some insight into the sources of the anger, and have a less habitual reaction the next time that nerve is touched.

Throughout my life I have reacted in anger to communications from my intimate partner that I interpret as blame. After more than enough years of making myself miserable with this negative pattern, I could finally see that my anger reaction is wholly and completely mine. When Barbara would simply ask me to take out the garbage, I would hear, "Why haven't you taken out the garbage yet?", when that was not what she meant at all. Due to my angry reactivity, I would get defensive, and start an unnecessary and unproductive argument from that stance. It often caused a temporary, but substantial, disruption in the quality of our relationship.

Now I am resolved to simply experience my reactivity to feeling blamed, and not lash out verbally. As I do this more and more, the sensations that accompany my anger are sufficiently diminished, and I am now able simply to drop into the feelings and excavate their wisdom. The insight that consistently arises through this process is that my sensitivity and reactivity is a response to having been unjustly blamed too often in my childhood. The shift to owning my anger has been an enormous boon to our intimacy. We now have far less conflict between us, and I feel much better as that mountain of heat diminishes. Overall, there is more peaceful space in our home for intimacy and joy to flourish.

The great Mahatma Gandhi said about anger, "I have learned through bitter experience the one supreme lesson: to conserve my anger, and as heat conserved is transmitted into energy, even so our anger controlled can be transmitted into a power which can move the world."

Sadness often lies beneath anger. In Buddhist psychology anger is considered a secondary emotion, sadness being its underlying foundation. When that is the case, quieting oneself and sitting with anger will reveal its true source in sadness, which more readily allows insight and release.

Sadness, like the other foundation emotions, is easier for some to let in than others. In general, in American culture it is easier for women than men to allow their sadness; men have been socialized to deny it. "Cowboys don't cry," we tell our boy children. What a violation of our humanity! As a result, many men suffer from unprocessed sadness. In fact it is critically important for all of us, men and women alike, to feel our sadness over the many losses and disappointments that life inevitably brings. When sadness and its more gripping sister, grief, go unexperienced, our aliveness is diminished, and depression can result.

My client Gordon was willing to feel his sadness, and both relief and insight were the result. Gordon came to me because he felt he was closing down to and shutting off his wife Lani. At a deeper level he knew he loved Lani dearly, and his withdrawal confused him. He could not understand his paradoxical reaction, which caused him great distress. He came to explore this with me in the hope of finding some relief and a renewed sense of closeness with his intimate partner.

After some discussion of the ways in which Gordon was shutting out Lani physically and emotionally, I asked him to remember the last time he had this experience, then to sink totally into the feelings associated with it. What emerged was a strong sensation in his heart area. I asked him what he was feeling there and he replied, "a very deep sadness." I encouraged him to stay with the sadness rather than push it away or skid off of it as tends to be our habit, and therefore to see what the feelings would teach him about the sources of his reactions. After a time his face contorted slightly. When I asked what he was experiencing, he said, "Rage. This is embarrassing to say, but I think deep down I hate women. You always have to perform for them to be appreciated. I just want to be loved for who I am, not to have to ask for it or perform to prove I deserve it."

At this point Gordon was deep inside of himself, and he began to speak freely about how his ex-wife was cold and distant, and only came toward him with love when he did something for her, like fixing her car or making her dinner. Then Gordon slipped into a feeling state that combined both anger and sadness. He talked about how his mother was also cold and distant, demanding that he perform for her love. And worse, she would beat Gordon for what he saw as no good reason. In that moment

Gordon shouted at the top his lungs, "STOP!"—a command directed at his mother. There was a long silence, and the room filled with a feeling of awe and completion.

When Gordon emerged from his cocoon of feelings, he spoke of the wounding caused by these two women. He clearly recognized that the true source of his shutting-down response was not Lani, but an unconscious reaction to his ex-wife and mother. Gordon recognized that Lani was not at all like the two women who had set this reaction in motion. Lani was an accepting, loving woman. She did not demand that he perform for her love. She loved him dearly, even through this period of Gordon's distance. The process of seeing and fully acknowledging this conscious distinction through the mechanism of allowing himself to truly feel his sadness opened up the possibility for Gordon to change his behavior toward his present intimate partner. As he left the session, Gordon said to me, "Thanks for helping me unlock the door. I can work with this now, and I think I can let Lani back in."

Invariably, there is some level of release from discomfort and constriction when we allow ourselves to fully feel our sadness. The release results from the sadness coming to the surface, where it can be experienced, integrated, and completed. Otherwise, it is likely to remain in the unconscious field, where it can cloud our emotional lives into the future. Because many of our childhood wounds result in sadness, when that emotion arises in the present, feeling it fully is a chance to release the incomplete childhood hurt. With the insight of a creative genius, Oscar Wilde described this potential: "Where there is sadness there is holy ground."

Fear is a particularly difficult emotion to allow ourselves to feel fully. It is so powerful and uncomfortable that it is hard to stay connected to it without running away, pushing it away, or denying that it is even there. Courage, it is said, is not the lack of fear, but the ability to stay with the feeling of fear and still act. Unprocessed fear often transmutes into violence. It is the child-abuser and the wife-beater who, beneath their abuse and violence, are themselves scared children lashing out in a feeble attempt to assuage their pain.

I personally have found it especially difficult to stay with the unique combination of sensations we call fear. Unfortunately, this is not a value or skill I was taught in my childhood. It has taken a lifetime, and some difficult lessons, to develop even a modest level of courage. Fear is so unpleasant and sometimes so overwhelming to me that I feel desperate to escape it, as when I was suddenly faced with a serious health issue.

About five years ago I began to have difficulty getting my full breath when I went for my daily runs. I have been a long distance runner since I was 13 years old, so I was familiar with the quality of my respiration when I was fit and when I was not. This experience reflected neither state. I was experiencing a kind of limitation of breath that was different from a lack of fitness. Since I have a history of bronchitis, I wasn't terribly worried, and went to my doctor to have her prescribe something that would take care of this minor bronchial problem. After examining me, her surprising remark was a phrase one never wants to hear from a physician: "I'm concerned. You need more tests."

I immediately went into denial and refused to accept my doctor's view that there might be something significantly wrong with me. If I had taken her seriously, believing that I might have some grave health problem, then I would have had to confront a reality I was not prepared to face. I did not have the courage to do that. So, the story I made up for myself was that this doctor was too young and inexperienced, and did not know me sufficiently well to understand how healthy I really was. I would just get another opinion and everything would be fine.

I called my dear and trusted friend Billy, a doctor, and asked him to take a look at me and give me his opinion. I knew his judgment would be correct, and that it would validate my story that I was fine. I saw Billy at his house. After listening to my heart and lungs he asked me to do an informal stress test by walking briskly around the block. He then checked me again and uttered the same dreaded words: "I'm concerned. You need more tests." He then recommended that I proceed with the formal stress test my original doctor had ordered.

Still, I found a way to remain in blissful denial during the three-week period before I took the test. And when I did take it, despite the shortness of breath and chest pain I felt while on the treadmill, I was certain everything was fine. It always had been. When we finished and I stepped down from the machine, I fully expected a "clean bill of health." Unfortunately, that was not the case. The nurse administering the test, after reading the results, looked at me gravely and simply said, "I have to take this to a cardiologist." Those were my last moments in the fearless fog of denial. When the nurse returned, she led me into her office, sat me down, and said, "The test indicates ischemia. A diminished blood flow to the heart. Hardening of the arteries. We need to take this further." She continued, "I'm going to make you an appointment with the cardiologist for more testing. For now, take these pills." She handed me a bottle and a prescription for refills, then ushered me out.

At that point the dam broke. The truth made it through. There was something seriously wrong with my health, and I was going to have to face it. And face it I did; delusion was no longer an option. From that point forward, until I had an angiogram—a test that determines the extent of blockage in the arteries feeding the heart—I experienced bottomless fear.

All my life I had denied my vulnerability to disease and, even more irrationally, my mortality. I was now feeling the full weight of the terror my self-deception had succeeded in keeping at bay. I had always denied the inevitability of my own death, never sincerely facing the fundamental truth of it. Whenever the subject of death came up in a serious fashion, I avoided it. I made up a story that put my mortality far enough off into the future that it had no sense of reality, and magically believed it was true. The deep fear I felt for the three weeks before my angiogram grabbed me by the throat and forced me to see clearly a fundamental existential reality: sooner or later, I will die.

Subsequently, the angiogram revealed 90 to 99 percent blockage in three cardiac arteries. The cardiologist looked me in the eye as I lay on the table, and said with the cold clarity only a surgeon could muster, "You need heart surgery, my friend. And, you need it immediately." As I screamed out into the operating theatre, "Noooooo!", another level of denial was broken. Before the angiogram, I had created yet another story, supported by what I was calling my intuition, that though I might need some kind of procedure, I definitely would not need open-heart surgery. Perhaps a simple stint procedure, but definitely not surgery. Ultimately, I had quadruple bypass surgery. After a long and arduous recovery, I am back to full health, and am even running again on the mountain that I so dearly love.

One of the gifts of this situation was being forced into fully experiencing my fear. I was no longer able to evade it. During the period leading up to my angiogram, the Emotional Wisdom work I did revealed to me that a lot of my fear of the medical system stemmed from frightening surgical experiences I had gone through as a child. In the process, I saw that there was an unhealed part of me that, if it remained unconscious, might actually lead to a decision to deny life-saving medical intervention just to avoid the experience of being in that system again. This insight allowed me to make a commitment to myself that I would summon the courage to be there for myself, and to do what I needed to survive.

A further blessing of this experience was coming to accept the inevitability of my own death. It, of course, is not something I welcome, but something that simply *is*. As a result, I am less fearful now, having faced and burned off some of the peak fear. I feel more fully alive, appreciative of this life I have been given, and deeply grateful for my moment-to-moment existence. The experience of feeling my fear fully has enriched my life immeasurably. I feel freer, more open, and more alive truly knowing at a deep gut level that this life is limited, and therefore extremely precious.

This experience has had a positive impact on the quality of my intimate relationship with Barbara as well. I am so grateful to her for sharing that difficult time with me, standing by me through it, and helping me every step of the way. I now feel that the way I can return that gift is with constant kindness. Through this kindness and my enhanced ability to avoid negative reactivity, our intimacy has grown enormously.

The beneficial effect of finding the courage to feel fear was similarly demonstrated to me by a participant in one of our couples workshops, Gina, a medical social worker. Gina worked on a cancer ward, and was with death and dying all day. Ironically, she also had a strong fear of death. This double bind was causing her great distress.

I asked Gina to lie down on the floor and die: to act as if she were really dead, to feel her way into the reality of that experience. This, of course, was a difficult assignment. But Gina found the courage to simulate her own death. To magnify the feeling I placed a blanket over her, covering her from head to toe. We darkened the room, the group remained quiet, and for Gina all external stimuli were eliminated. Gina's first reaction was terror. She began to tremble, and the trembling spread over her whole body. Then she screamed in protest, but managed to stay with the process. After two minutes these reactions began to subside and gradually fade away. She relaxed. Within five minutes Gina reported that she was experiencing total ease. When I asked her how she was experiencing herself, she simply said, "free." She felt released. Having allowed herself to actually experience and feel her fear of death instead of living in a constant state of pushing it away, Gina came to rest. Her willingness to simulate death, ride the whole wave of emotion from its initial phases to its apex, then down to its nadir, was a deeply healing event.

As a continuing participant in the ongoing couples workshop, Gina reported that this Emotional Wisdom work had freed her to be more comfortable on the job and more effective with her clients. Even years later she continued to feel at ease, open, and available to her ill and dying clients. The work also had a salutary effect on her intimate relationship. Her husband, also in the group, reported that now when Gina returned home from work she was more energetic and available to him and their daughter. The intimacy between all members of her family grew as a result of her personal Emotional Wisdom work. This kind of outcome is typical. Any growth work we do to free ourselves from habitual constrictions and negative reactivity will support the growth of intimacy in our relationship.

Joy, the final of our foundational emotions, should be the emotion easiest to experience. After all, as animals, our natural tendency is to seek pleasure and avoid pain. Certainly for most people it is far easier to let happiness in than the challenging emotions of anger, sadness, and fear. However, as we humans are a unique breed, letting joy in is not always easy. For some, it is so far from their habitual experience that the emotion of happiness is both scary and difficult to fully embrace.

A friend's friend married a young woman who had been sexually abused as a child. She became a prostitute as a teenager, and had major difficulties with substance abuse. She had experienced much horror and unhappiness in her life. Through a series of unusual and fortunate circumstances, she met and married a man who was kind, responsible, and very loving. They had a child, bought a beautiful house in a lovely neighborhood, and appeared to have a very happy life together. Yet, after only two years, she left. Apparently she could not handle the joy of her new life. It was too unfamiliar. And because of its unfamiliarity, it was too uncomfortable for her to bear. She simply could not allow herself to experience the joy. She had to avoid it and change her entire life to get away from feeling the discomfort of happiness.

Joy is not just a lollipop that one experiences for its pleasure alone. Joy holds the potential for release and insight as well. The physician Bernie Siegel proved the healing power of laughter, and spread the word throughout our society in his popular book, *Love, Medicine, and Miracles.* Joy helps get us in touch with our true priorities. Looking into the eyes of our children, deeply connecting with our partner, listening to the sound of water in a stream, we appreciate the preciousness of the moment we are given. We appreciate the gift of Life and the foolishness of wasting it on petty matters. It is a reminder of what is really meaningful, and of the central importance of gratitude and kindness. It is a reminder of the truth in the cliché, "No one has ever written on their tombstone, I wish I had spent more time at the office."

Unfortunately, many people in our society have an aversion to fully experiencing their emotions. Besides the culturally conditioned tendency to ignore one's feelings, many believe that if they were to begin to open up to their emotions, they could not stop the torrent to follow. They fear that the flood would incapacitate them, that the faucet would never turn off. It would pour out endlessly, and they would be disabled in the world. This belief is understandable because those trained not to feel have a vast backlog of unexpressed feelings. The prospect of opening up that backlog is terrifying. It would mean entering unknown territory that has been avoided, and facing the scary monster in the basement. We fear that if we were to look at it, we would be extinguished. Exactly the opposite is true. Looking squarely at the monster, allowing it to climb out of the basement, gives us information critical to our wellbeing. As the poet Rainer Maria Rilke wrote, "Perhaps everything terrible is in its deepest being something terrible that wants help from us."

I have worked with numerous people, men and women alike, who initially would not allow themselves to cry. Upon examination, they reveal that they fear that if they were to allow themselves to begin crying, the tears would never cease. They worry that they have so much sadness within that its thirst for expression is unquenchable. They must hold it back with a dike of avoidance and denial. Imagine how difficult it is for a person to carry all that grief and fear when the outlet, the healing agent of release through the cleansing power of tears, is not available. Then imagine how much irrational and unproductive behavior such an approach engenders, and how much suffering it causes to the people close by. As Arnold Mindell, a gifted psychiatrist, described it, "Devaluing feelings and just letting them go is like tossing wastepaper on the street. Somebody has to clean it up eventually."

If, as a facilitator, I can create an emotionally safe environment and guide such people into the unknown territory of their feelings, though their tears may be many, they often find that there is an end to the sadness, and the release is ecstatic. When sadness and grief are not experienced, when their associated feelings are not felt, what typically emerges is a flatness of affect, often a state of depression that follows from capping our natural aliveness. Anger denied can turn to rage that emerges unwanted, creating destructive cycles of attack and defense, undermining the intimacy we desire. Fear unfelt can lead to nervousness and free-floating anxiety. It does not allow the full appreciation of the joy of living, and the delight of our senses. Sound, sight, and sensation are dulled by unexperienced fear, which can turn into an enveloping state of apprehension. So no matter how challenging, it is better for the quality of our life and the quality of our relationship that we move from denial of our emotions to truly experiencing our feelings; that we move into an appreciation of Emotional Wisdom, so that we learn how to work with feelings and heal through them.

Just as some try to ignore their feelings only to create blocks in their intimacy, others hide behind a spiritual attitude, asserting that if they are sufficiently dedicated to a spiritual path, emotional work is not necessary. Though this may be accurate as a theoretical proposition and true for a very small number of people, it remains an excuse for denial in the vast majority of cases. With the exception of a handful of spiritual masters, I have not met anyone who is clear enough at the personality level not to be reactive and in need of emotional as well as spiritual wisdom. The alternative to this evasion is beautifully expressed by the Buddhist teacher Pema Chodron: "In the process of discovering our true nature, the journey goes down, not up ... Instead of transcending the suffering of all creatures, we move toward the turbulence and doubt ... We explore the reality and unpredictability of insecurity and pain and we try not to push it away."[3] Or, as Arnold Mindell expressed it, "Long ago I dreamed that the Buddha said that if process work *[Emotional Wisdom work in our terms]* had been available in his day he would have used it, because it is an express train to the same spot."

The psychological and spiritual teacher A.H. Almaas also offered an on-the-mark description of this process in an interview with Tony Schwartz: "...because ego or personality is so incredibly entrenched— because people's unconscious fears and conflicts so stand in their way— meditative practices are rarely sufficient as a route to recovering one's true nature in everyday life. Many people do a great deal of meditation, only to remain stuck in their personalities, unable to let go of their fixations. The way we get to our essential nature is not primarily through spiritual exercises, but through psychological work to penetrate parts of the personality that are connected to underlying essential aspects of ourselves. Psychological inquiry leads to spiritual realization. Meditation supports this inquiry and sharpens it, but the psychological work is inseparable from the spiritual practice."[4]

Two colorful and useful metaphors can help us better grasp and remember the value of Emotional Wisdom work. These are:

- Emotional Wisdom as a *birthing process*, much like being in the delivery room for new life. It is painful, confusing, sometimes far too slow, and other times far too fast for our comfort. Yet the outcome is the beauty and joy of new life, an occasion for gratitude and celebration.

- Emotional Wisdom as a *process of breaking into prison*. This means going into a restrictive, uncomfortable territory, yet coming out (unlike most prison experiences) a rehabilitated, wiser, and far better person.

Finally, there is a lovely poem by the Frenchman Guillaume Apollinaire that sums it up:

> *Come to the edge, he said.*
> *They said: We are afraid.*
> *Come to the edge, he said.*
> *They came.*
> *He pushed them ...*
> *and they flew*

10 ❧ Jumping In

All suffering comes from wanting it to be some way other than the way it is. The end of suffering is surrendering to what is.

As we have seen, developing and sustaining intimacy is fundamentally an "inside job." It is a process centered on one's connection with oneself. It also requires a willingness to truly *Jump In*, to fully commit to relationship. It is giving a resounding "Yes!" to the intimate dimension. It does not mean giving up oneself to the other person. It does mean allowing one's resistance to yield to giving oneself fully to relationship. As in the world of finance, *yield* here also means reward and gain.

Though a healthy life requires a balance between autonomy and connectedness, we often behave in ways that appear to support our sense of autonomy, but which are actually habitual protective responses that damage the connection with our partner. Finding the proper balance between autonomy and connectedness is a challenge. Those who hold too tightly to autonomy will not find intimacy, because from this position there is not sufficient openness for deep connection. Those who nurture only belonging will not find intimacy, because from this stance there is no one there for the other to be intimate with.

Again and again I see people in relationship who are adamant about maintaining their autonomy, even when there is no real threat to it. Their independence is not in danger, yet they are unyielding in their defense of it. It would appear that they "protest too much." They do not have a strong enough sense of independence to withstand intimate relationship. In an attempt to bolster this weakness, they refuse to enter into full connection. From this place of insecurity an unconscious Core Belief can emerge: "if I give myself to the other, I will be lost." The "I" fears it will lose itself in the abyss of "Other." In a couple, creating distance from one's partner in order to bolster this sense of separateness often manifests over time in an unsatisfying sexual relationship. If one cannot surrender to the relationship, how can one expect a partner to surrender to the vulnerability and depth that true sexual connection requires?

Many relationship theorists emphasize the *autonomy* component of the autonomy/connectedness polarity. I believe that is because most of us come to relationship without having done the individual work necessary to sufficiently develop our emotional maturity. Under these conditions, if we were to emphasize the *surrender* component, we might fall prey to codependence: the condition of trying to live life through the other. This pattern inhibits both personal growth and intimacy.

In a life fully lived, one that includes physical, mental, emotional, and spiritual practice, along with the maturity that this personal work produces, it is possible to jump into relationship without codependence. We need to be strong enough and individuated enough to successfully yield to connection.

The inability to fully jump in and release our resistance to relationship is at the heart of the so-called "commitment problem," where one partner, most often the man, appears not to be willing to "commit" to the relationship. If we emphasize the verb form, "committing," rather than the noun, "commitment," focusing on process rather than on outcome, a more successful orientation for building intimacy is gained. Committing is a moment-to-moment practice. It is a development, an unfolding of allegiance to another, not turning a switch from off to on, once and for all. It is a series of actions, not a fixed position. Committing is the choice, over and over again, to offer up to the other the gift of our time, energy, and devotion. It is the choice to share our inner experience with the other. To choose actions that are kind and that bring pleasure to our partner. Intimacy grows naturally out of this rich soil of committing.

Thought of in another way, for a man, he is not committing to the woman, but to the feminine principle within himself. For a woman, she is not committing to the man, but to the male within. For both, this means opening to the part of oneself that is less dominant and in the background, thereby becoming more integrated and whole. This is not a loss of self or one's integrity. This is not the cynical, "yes, honey" of the television situation comedies. It is much deeper than that. It involves not a deficit of integrity, but a gain in it. It is a gentle taming of the dominant ego: the immature ego that must have its way at the expense of the quality of the bond or the true quality of one's own life.

Jumping In is really a kind of acceptance of what committing is. In that way it is a spiritual practice. It is accepting our partner as they are rather than trying to make them into who or what we want them to be. It is relinquishing a harmful sense of control over the other. Jumping In is about victory: the victory of the connection and what it brings to the lives of the individuals who are connected.

Jumping In is also a psychological practice: giving up the limitations and reactivity of the conditioned personality. It means being aware enough to notice the habit patterns that motivate us to want to control or change our partner. It also means being clear enough to choose not to act out of those habits, but to behave from a place of spaciousness and ease, a place that knows that nurturing the relationship is nurturing oneself.

Jumping In is a form of generosity, a bighearted willingness to give. It displays nobility of character, a generous and kind spirit.

For health, there is a need for balance. Jumping In to relationship just to have a relationship is not healthy. A Jumping In that does not honor the self, that is in fact a giving up of oneself, loving in order to avoid loneliness by maintaining a relationship at any cost, is a losing proposition. We cannot gain intimacy with another at the expense of intimacy with our self.

Jumping In to relationship in the positive sense is a series of giving up negatives and acquiring positives. It is giving up limitation, reactivity, the need to be right, the need to dominate, the struggle for power, possessing or claiming the other, the need to subordinate, the need to get one's own way. It is committing on a moment-to-moment basis to being your highest and best self.

11 ❧ Gratitude and Kindness

Gratitude is the only prayer I know.
OSHO

My religion is kindness.
THE DALAI LAMA

When I had heart surgery everything changed. Before, my relationship with Barbara was good; now it is great. This has happened because of gratitude and kindness. While I was in long-term physical and emotional recovery, I learned one of the defining lessons of my life: the centrality of gratitude in creating a happy life and a loving relationship.

Two weeks after my surgery, when I was newly home and still very much in the thrall of the experience, my dear friends Billy and Merv came to visit. I remember telling them with wet eyes, "After all the fear and pain, after the loss of cherished concepts and faith, all that is left is gratitude and love." I felt deep gratitude for my life, for my wife, for my family, my daughter, my friends, and all the gifts of creation. The scent of wind through the window as I sat in our bed and read. The sound of the earth crackling under my feet as I took my first steps outside. The moment-to-moment deliciousness of sensory awareness.

What grew within me most, and keeps growing, is my gratitude to Barbara, who lovingly nursed me back to health. Barbara, who was there for me through my long and tortuous post-surgical depression. Barbara, who so kindly sustained me through my pain. I have seen clearly through the example of my own life that gratitude is a powerful force for generating, mobilizing, and sustaining intimacy.

I heard recently of a study comparing people who had won the lottery to people who had survived a life-threatening accident. The latter group emerged far happier. The reason that so many are transformed for the better after surviving a life-threatening experience is that gratitude for life becomes predominant.

It is a worthy intention to support and grow this inclination toward gratitude without the necessity of experiencing a dire threat to our mortality. How does one develop this level of gratitude without suffering a life-threatening experience? Truly, I have not found a sufficiently satisfying answer. My best conclusion is that the simplest way we can learn to nourish gratitude is through the intentional development of awareness and choice. In particular, we can grow gratitude through consciously choosing to be aware of the gifts that are brought to us through the doorway of our senses: slowing down and noticing the exquisite beauty of sight, sound, smell, touch, and taste. Then, by focusing our awareness on the natural, but buried, background appreciation we feel for receiving the gift of this delicious beauty, we bring it to the foreground and drop into the full experience of gratitude. Gratitude for the gifts of the senses naturally evolves to a larger gratitude, especially appreciation for our intimate partner, the person who has given us the greatest gift a person can give: the gift of their life companionship.

The cultivation of gratitude can be understood as a practice, one in which from time to time we intentionally bring to awareness our appreciation for all that we have, including our appreciation for our partner. Gratitude holds the magic to transform our connection into a deeper, more satisfying, more intimate relationship. One very good way of practicing gratitude is to intentionally focus our first thoughts upon arising toward appreciation. As an alternative to staying with worry or planning, we can shift our focus to giving thanks for another day of life, for our partner, for any and all the things that enrich our life. This simple act brings vitality and joy to the day.

Taking ourselves into Nature is another practice that inspires gratitude. The awesome beauty of the forest, the oceans, the mountains, or a simple field of grass opens us up to gratitude. We can go outside and take a Gratitude Walk: a walk in which we hold gratitude in the forefront as our constant companion. There is both an enlivening and calming quality to this experience. A lightness results, which brings happiness to our life.

Another way to cultivate gratitude is to develop a set of *Stillpoints*. These are ordinary, repetitive moments in our lives in which we consciously stop our activity and give ourselves over fully to appreciation. We select as reminders common experiences in our day-to-day lives and use them as Stillpoints. We can choose the most mundane, repetitive moments to trigger our gratitude, such as the moment before we answer the phone or the moment of opening a door. We can give ourselves over to gratitude while standing in line waiting as an alternative to impatience and discomfort. A very inspiring young couple we know stops every evening at 6 p.m. to give thanks for all their blessings. I see that they have enriched their lives and their relationship through this practice.

A poem by Hafiz beautifully encapsulates this attitude:

> *Slipping*
> *On my shoes,*
> *Boiling water,*
> *Toasting bread,*
> *Buttering the sky:*
> *That should be enough contact*
> *With God in one day*
> *To make anyone*
> *Crazy.*[5]

And again, there is the practice of cultivating sensory awareness. Sensory awareness not only nourishes gratitude, it creates a positive cycle of joy. The practice of gratitude brings us to the present and provides an opening to the joy of the senses. When we are worrying, planning, or focusing on the past or future, we are not available for the exquisite feedback possible from our senses, and our sense receptors become dulled. When we are in gratitude, our senses become highly refined. Without the need to choose, we experience our sight more vividly, our hearing more acutely, our smell more sensitively, our taste more fully, while the touch of our partner becomes a deep delight.

Gratitude lends a feeling of inner strength, spaciousness, and freedom, whatever the status of our external circumstances. It engenders an attitude of expectancy and receptivity, which increases the probability of receiving from our partner and others what we desire for our self. Gratitude helps us really experience—not just at the cognitive level, but deep down—the preciousness of this life we are given. It helps us to feel how fleeting this happiness is, and how easily it can go away. It helps us understand that there are no guarantees, that the gifts of our senses, our partner, our friends and family, might not last any longer than this moment, that it might be gone the next. And that knowing, though bittersweet, is central to leading a fulfilled life.

Kindness is the currency of gratitude. It is the behavior that is capable of expressing the thankfulness we feel for the other. In my case, it became clear to me that I was so full of gratitude for Barbara's compassion, that simple justice required I become more aware of my unkind behaviors and more committed to kindness in word and deed. As a result, I have transformed from a partner whose behavior could be testy and mean when I felt grumpy, to one who can still feel grumpy, but who most often does not pass on that discomfort through my behavior. Now when I feel cranky, I am more aware of it. Instead of unconsciously spilling out my inner discomfort in meanness, I can choose to keep my irritability within, remaining externally kind despite my mood.

Kindness is a way of honoring our partner for sharing their one precious life with us. It is a way to balance the scales for their commitment and willingness to be with us through the vicissitudes of this life: through sickness and health, richer and poorer, and all the rest.

Surprisingly, what we discovered in our relationship was that most of Barbara's unkindness towards me was reactive. It was an unconscious response to my unkind behavior toward her. When my gratitude grew and more kindness emerged, the kindness came back to me from her. This is an example of a fundamental law of human systems: when one element in the system changes (in this example, my behavior), the whole system shifts. It also explains why it is such a poor and inevitably frustrating choice to wait for our partner to change in order to increase the intimacy in the relationship. If we change our self in a direction that supports intimacy, it will inevitably grow the bond.

My gratitude toward Barbara seems to be a state into which I have permanently shifted. I am so aware that because she is my life companion, I value her too much for unkindness. Though I sometimes fail in this effort, I am aware of the failure. I usually apologize and internally recommit to an effort to achieve kindness.

To become more kind to our partner we need not try to figure out every little piece of behavior that might constitute kindness. The key is to commit to kindness deep down at the attitudinal level, invite kindness into the guts of our belief system. If we truly incorporate gratitude at the attitudinal level, the correct behavior will naturally flow from it. It will come from a deep, positive place.

Viktor Frankl's observation about the power of attitude in the worst possible circumstances is an eloquent testament to this: "We who lived in concentration camps can remember the men who walked through the huts comforting others, giving away their last piece of bread. They may have been few in number, but they offer sufficient proof that everything can be taken away from a man but one thing; the last of the human freedoms—to choose one's attitude in any given set of circumstances, to choose our own way."[6]

It is important to distinguish between being kind and being nice. Niceness is constructed, conditional behavior. It is designed to generate a predicted positive response from the other. Kindness is unconditional. It is not about generating a return. Its intention is directed toward the well-being of the other, and its reward lies in its intrinsic joy. Kindness is abundantly generous. A fundamental component of kindness is the willingness to suspend one's self-interest long enough to listen empathetically and non-judgmentally. In this way kindness is not only an act of sympathy and compassion, but a healing agent as well—a medicine for one's emotional wounding. Stated in its strongest form by the psychologist John Firman in his book, *The Primal Wound*, "The cause of primal wounding lies not in the suffering itself, but in the absence of some empathetic other, and thus the threat of non-being. Without this kind of listening, the very oxygen source for one's being is threatened and we face a headlong fall out of the universe, a plunge into nothingness."[7]

Similarly, as our friend Peter Frieberg said to us in one of our recent workshops, "We are all at the deepest level like light. In order to see ourselves, it has to be reflected off of others or we can't really know who we are."

Kindness implies the willingness to forgive. Forgiveness for some of us is extremely difficult. We hold white-knuckled onto our anger and resentment as if it were the source of our safety. This, of course, is an illusion. Clinging to our anger is actually a weight pulling us under. What is there to forgive, after all? In most cases, with the exception of those rare occasions when we are truly violated, most of the anger and resentment we are unwilling to release is based upon our own internal dynamics rather than on the object of our anger. We are disturbed because something within us is triggered by the other. And it is that place within us that needs healing and forgiveness more than the other person.

I held a grudge against a dean of a university where I worked because I felt he disrespected me. He did not honor me enough not to try to change me into his image of what a professor should be. After months of internal agonizing, I realized it was I who did not honor myself enough not to try to change me. Once I understood this, my feeling about the dean became neutralized. I no longer felt charged when I saw or thought of him, and I experienced myself as less constricted and more spacious. Not forgiving is not only unkind to the other, it is unkind to ourselves. Holding on to resentment and anger rather than letting it go is, as the old adage states, "like taking poison and hoping the other person dies."

Acceptance is gratitude in action. Like kindness, acceptance of our partner, without any effort to change them or make them different, is another currency of gratitude. It is a way of honoring our partner and sending the message that they are fine just as they are.

Of course, to accept others requires that we first accept ourselves. This is a challenging proposition. Most of us were raised with large doses of criticism. We received countless messages, both overt and covert, that we are not good enough the way we are. We were asked to change in some direction that allowed our parents and others in authority to feel more comfortable with their own unexamined selves. Even in those cases where the intention was to "make us better people," the deeper outcome was to inculcate in us a sense of unworthiness and self-rejection. So, to offer the currency of acceptance to our partner is to give the gift of gratitude as a remedy for the effects of those lifelong harmful messages.

There is an entire school of psychotherapy based on gratitude. It is called Naikan, or "looking inside therapy." It is Japanese in origin, and its intent is to help heal emotional wounding through bringing to consciousness how blessed we are, to make gratitude an active process in the forefront of our thinking. In this interpersonally-focused therapeutic model, when looking at people in our lives against whom we are reacting, we are directed to not ask, "what's wrong with them?", or "how can I change them?", or even "what's wrong with me?", but to ask the following three questions:

1. What have I received from this person?

2. What have I given this person?

3. What difficulties have I caused this person?

With the Naikan approach we bring forth our gratitude and look for the currency with which to compensate the other for the difficulties we have inevitably caused them.

As a friend recently said to her husband of 35 years while discussing this subject, "Gratitude makes me happy. Kindness makes you happy." What a lovely basis for long-term intimacy.

12 ✧ Mature Love

Love is much nicer to be in than an automobile accident, a tight girdle,
a higher tax bracket or a holding pattern over Philadelphia.

JUDITH VIORST

R *omantic Love* is a beautiful experience. It lifts us to the heights. The feeling of "being in love" is similar to the bliss of Divine connection. "Falling in love" is marked by excitement, intensity, and a strong sexual pull. It is often accompanied by a sense that, "at last my life is fulfilled." Yet Romantic Love, in its initial blind, blissful, and crazy phase, must evolve into a more ripened form of love, one that is more substantial if it is to endure in the long run. Love limited to romance alone is not enough to sustain a satisfying long-term intimate relationship. Romantic Love in its most useful form is a doorway to Mature Love.

The drive towards Romantic Love and its idealization as the Holy Grail of life is one of the most emphasized and deeply imbedded messages in our society. Its praises are expressed everywhere, in most every form of art and media. We are conditioned to believe that this very pleasing, indefinable feeling we call Romantic Love is the missing element that will create happiness in our lives. We are everywhere urged to seek love. It is so widely and strongly emphasized that few of us even question Romantic Love's true nature and proper place in the development of a healthy intimate relationship.

The phenomenon we call Romantic Love may, in actuality, be a highly combustible mix of two elements: projection and lust. Lust, the physical component, is a powerful sexual drive biologically programmed within us. And projection, as we have seen, is the complex psychological process by which we see in others the qualities we do not see or accept in ourselves.

In the initial phases of Romantic Love it is predominantly our "light" qualities that are projected. We cast out our own positive characteristics, which we do not see in our self, but recognize through the mirroring offered by the other. This positive mirroring from the object of our Romantic Love creates an enormously powerful attraction. We are seeing the best of our self in our partner. Romantic Love, as magnificent as it is, is in large part a process involving sexual arousal and falling in love with oneself.

Unfortunately, if we cling to this process, inevitably the "shadow projections" will show up. These are negative qualities in our self, which we do not like, and do not want to see. As the pendulum begins to swing back over time, we increasingly see these unappealing qualities in our beloved. As a result, judgment, aversion, resentment, and animosity arise.

True Love, Love with a capital "L," is developmental. It has stages of growth like all living processes. Just as Life must progress from the egg to the embodied being, Love must move beyond its initial romantic form if it is to stay alive. Romantic Love must develop into Mature Love for it to reach its fullness and richness. The greatest gift Romantic Love can offer us is a beginning, a doorway to the deeper, more enduring satisfaction of Mature Love.It is vital for intimate partners, after experiencing the beauty and joy of Romantic Love, to find their way into Mature Love, to evolve from the embryonic state into the developed state. As the author Ursula Le Guin notes "Love doesn't just sit there like a stone, it has to be made, like bread, remade all the time, made new." So, how do we make our Love anew? What does Mature Love look like? The purpose of this book is to paint that picture. Mature Love is the couple walking down the path of Life together, holding hands, supporting each other in their growth and healing. This is not a new perspective. Margaret Fuller wrote of it in a book entitled *Women in the Nineteenth Century*, published in 1845. She said that intimate relationship in its highest form is "a pilgrimage of two souls toward a common shrine."

Mature Love becomes possible as we cultivate Self-Love. To cultivate self-love we must cultivate self-acceptance and non-judgment of our self. Without these qualities, any consistent level of acceptance of our partner is impossible to achieve. And without acceptance we fall short of truly loving our partner.

Conversely, the absence of self-love and self-acceptance is self-rejection. Self-rejection is a culturally conditioned state in which we often unconsciously reside. From this harsh and unforgiving position of mind, how is it possible for us to accept the other? And if our partner does not feel accepted, how can they feel loved? The Acceptance/Rejection polarity is a key dynamic in determining the quality of relationships. Acceptance and rejection of our self and our partner is not a black and white matter. We live and think along a continuum, with acceptance at one end, and rejection at the other. The conditioning to judge is too deeply ingrained for us to think we can eliminate it entirely. The work is to move ourselves incrementally toward the acceptance end of the continuum by becoming aware of our conditioned tendency toward judgment, and choosing acceptance as a positive alternative.

The origins of self-judgment and consequent self-rejection can be found at the macroscopic level in the widespread belief in Western culture that we improve through criticism. This belief is dropped on us by the authority figures in our lives, mainly parents, older siblings, teachers, and bosses. After years and years of being criticized "for our own good" and "to make us better people," we do what in psychology is called introject. That is, we take the voices of others and make them our own. We mercilessly criticize ourselves as if we have taken the audiotape of our parents, teachers, and bosses, running it on continuous play in our own minds. Now we no longer need "them" to criticize us; we do it to ourselves.

The sad fallacy in this culturally generated assumption that criticism is the mainspring of improvement is that while it may at times be effective in producing some desired short-term outcome, it comes at too high a cost. The price is self-rejection, and ultimately the learned rejection of the other. Beyond that, this compulsion towards criticism in many ways does not produce improvement. When we are judged, the contraction we experience throws us into defense. From a defensive posture it is hard to change. The behavior, which in fact may need altering, is frozen in place, and we lose the ability to alter it.

Conversely, when we feel accepted we can more easily notice a behavior that is not working for us, and we have the internal freedom to change that behavior in a direction we prefer. This has been demonstrated literally millions of times in the area of weight loss. Those of us who criticize and reject our bodies for being fat seldom succeed in losing weight. Those who first learn to accept their body as it is are more successful in achieving the goal of weight reduction.

There are a number of habits of mind that block us from allowing self-acceptance. There is the comfortable familiarity we have after many years with self-judgment sitting on our shoulder. It is not a happy state, but it is a well-known one. There is a sense of safety in it, a satisfying stability. The thought of changing any mental pattern, including moving from self-judgment to self-acceptance, can bring up fear of the unknown. We habitually avoid fear, so we may habitually avoid self-acceptance.

Also, many of us fear that if we were to be kind, non-judgmental, and self-accepting, we would get nothing done. Lethargy, apathy, and sloth would predominate. This is an unfortunate illusion because, as we discussed earlier, self-acceptance is energizing, and actually enables improvement.

For some there is an even bigger fear, one akin to a sense of impending doom. If we were to accept ourselves, we think, "The entire foundation upon which my life has been constructed might come tumbling down. Chaos might ensue, and I could be annihilated." Though this may sound exaggerated, it is not uncommon for us fallible humans to have that level of fear about letting go of a Core Belief.

One of self-judgment's most unpleasant attributes is the sense of bodily constriction or compression it generates. It is not the initial discernment of our own behavior as wrong or inappropriate that is so hurtful to ourselves. This first discernment is a simple recognition that our behavior was not what we would have preferred to choose. It is the secondary level of judgment, the self-criticism, the act of proceeding to make ourselves wrong, that is so harmful. This level of judgment causes a compression in the body, and a diminishment in our sense of self.

For example, I say something unkind to my wife. I notice that my words were unkind and that I don't like what I said. I would have preferred to behave differently. That level of self-reflection may be called discernment. Insight at this level is healthy, and supports me in becoming more who I want to be.

It is the secondary process that is so self-immolating: when I proceed to say to myself, "Oh shit! What an ass I am. I've done it again. When will I ever learn?", or something of that nature. This second level is not only harmful to myself, it puts me in an even more foul mood, making it more likely that I will consciously or unconsciously continue to be unkind in my behavior. This type of thinking creates constriction and compression, which minimizes my flexibility to change my behavior going forward. When we are compressed, it is difficult to be kind to others, and it is potentially damaging to the long-term quality of our relationships. Self-forgiveness is a decompressing process. It literally takes the pressure off the body and allows a more expansive mental state. We feel better, and we are better able to change our behavior. When I spoke harshly to my wife, if I had subsequently been able to skip the "Oh shit! What an ass I am ..." part, and simply recognized the error of my ways, I would have been more likely to apologize. And I subsequently would have felt more empowered to avoid the same pattern in the future.

The secondary self-criticism is most always self-flagellation. Removing this level of judgment from our habitual thinking process is the antidote to the compression. Noticing the self-rejection and letting it go without believing it or buying into its story creates interior space. We feel expanded and light. More free. From this place of expansion, lightness, and freedom, we are naturally lovers.

The strength of these blocks and the challenges they create reveals that although self-acceptance is a necessary component for truly loving another human being, it is a difficult pose to hold. My great and gifted teacher, Harry Sloan, emphasized the healing quality of allowing. I can see him in my mind's eye in a group therapy process. Someone is expressing their pain, and Harry rises from his chair and comes toward them to help. He moves slowly and easily, emanating a quality of gentleness. He says, "Allow this. Allow this. Allow this." The person relaxes, and half the work is already done. Those simple words, which encourage self-acceptance, enable the person to relax, open up, and prepare to go to a deeper level of healing.

Another great therapist and teacher, Dick Olney, went so far in his belief that self-acceptance was the core psychological process for mental health that by the end of his career he was calling his entire body of work "Self-Acceptance Training."

A particularly vulnerable time for self-judgment is when we are feeling sad, or what we sometimes call depressed. We are culturally conditioned to believe we "should" be happy, to believe that there is some moral failure in being sad. When we feel sad, we judge ourselves harshly. "Why aren't I happy? There must be something wrong with me." Making wrong the experience of feeling sad is like making the rain wrong. It may be unpleasant, but it is natural and real. Sadness is as much a naturally occurring reality as joy. To reject ourselves for feeling blue generates the tertiary phenomenon of compression, which is damaging to our spirit. When sadness arises, the skillful thing to do is to allow it. Allow it, feel it fully, and honor its presence until it passes. Just as the rain recedes and the sunshine shows up, sadness will pass away naturally.

Although difficult, it is possible to unlearn self-judgment and self-criticism, and to learn self-acceptance. More than anything else, this requires an attitudinal shift: a belief that leads to a desire to drop the self-defeating practice, overcome the habit and blocks, and generate a willingness to be self-accepting. I would like to offer an effective process for making the transition from self-rejection to self-acceptance. It may be summarized as the *Three R's: Recognize, Release* and *Reprogram.*

Recognition is the first step. It requires the cultivation of moment-to-moment awareness. Because the habit is so deeply ingrained, we are seldom actually fully aware that we are judging and rejecting ourselves. It is happening on automatic pilot. The antidote to being a prisoner of the mind's unconscious process is an awareness of what our mind is actually doing, which requires close attention. We note the signals in the body, particularly those of constriction or compression. This often shows up in the chest, belly, or jaw, but can occur anywhere in the body. By noting these signals we recognize that self-judging and self-rejecting is happening.

The skill of developing acute moment-to-moment awareness of self requires practice. A good way to learn is to study and practice some form of awareness-oriented meditation: sitting quietly and noting what is going on in the mind and body. Doing this will eventually carry over into daily life, and we become more able to recognize our negative self-judgment.

The second step in moving from self-judgment to self-acceptance is Release. Releasing the negative habitual pattern of self-condemnation. The mechanics of this step may feel counterintuitive to some. It requires going deeply into the feelings associated with the judgment and experiencing them fully. As described in the chapter on Emotional Wisdom, this process will reveal insights into the origins of our self-judgments and provide some level of release from its stranglehold.

Finally, there is Reprogramming. This is the phase of positively choosing self-acceptance and self-love. It is the step where, after having recognized our habit of self-judgment and gaining some insight into its genesis, we make a different choice. We choose self-love. If we become skillful enough, we can choose self-acceptance when we notice the bodily constriction and the presence of self-criticism. We treat these cues like a monk treats the temple bell that calls him to prayer. We feel the constriction and take that as the bell that calls us to automatically move toward self-acceptance.

This alternative is not easy. With a lifetime devoted to self-disapproval, and the deep rut it has driven into our psyche, it requires a great effort of will to change, to backfill that groove and make a field of Love. The movement from self-denunciation to self-embrace, the expansiveness it engenders, the lightness it offers, is enormously liberating and energizing, a reward well worth the challenge.

Total self-acceptance is total self-transformation. A Sufi story paints this picture beautifully. Once a young woman asked Hafiz, the Persian poet of Divine Love, "What is the sign of someone knowing God?" Hafiz replied, "They have dropped the knife. The cruel knife we use upon our tender self and others."

Below is an email that someone sent me, which they found on the web. It has some sage advice on Love from 4- to 8-year-old children. A group of them was asked, "What does love mean?" Here are some of their answers:

"When my grandmother got arthritis, she couldn't bend over and paint her toenails anymore. So my grandfather does it for her all the time, even when his hands got arthritis too. That's love."

(Rebecca, age 8)

"When someone loves you, the way they say your name is different. You just know that your name is safe in their mouth."

(Billy, age 4)

"Love is when you go out to eat and give somebody most of your French fries without making them give you any of theirs."

(Chris, age 6)

"Love is when my mommy makes coffee for my daddy and she takes a sip before giving it to him, to make sure the taste is OK."

(Danny, age 7)

"Love is when you kiss all the time. Then when you get tired of kissing, you still want to be together and you talk more."

(Emily, age 8)

"Love is what's in the room with you at Christmas if you stop opening presents and listen."

(Bobby, age 7)

"If you want to learn to love better, you should start with a friend who you hate."

(Nikka, age 6)

"Love is when you tell a guy you like his shirt, then he wears it every day."

(Noelle, age 7)

"Love is like a little old woman and a little old man who are still friends even after they know each other so well."

(Tommy, age 6)

"During my piano recital, I was on a stage and I was scared. I looked at all the people watching me and saw my daddy waving and smiling. He was the only one doing that. I wasn't scared any more."

(Cindy, age 8)

"Love is when Mommy gives Daddy the best piece of chicken."

(Elaine, age 5)

"Love is when Mommy sees Daddy smelly and sweaty and still says he is handsomer than Robert Redford."

(Chris, age 7)

"Love is when your puppy licks your face even after you left him alone all day."

(Mary Ann, age 4)

"You really shouldn't say 'I love you' unless you mean it. But if you mean it, you should say it a lot. People forget."

(Jessica, age 8)

13 ∞ Communication

Our society has spent so much time and achieved such startling results with the discovery of new mechanical processes of communication, but we have somehow forgotten that the process of living demands the ability to respond, to make contact, and to communicate one's experience to another human being.

LEE STRASBERG (*A DREAM OF PASSION*)

In relationship, communication serves as both prevention and cure. Properly employed, communication minimizes conflict and provides a vehicle for resolving it when conflict does occur.

As prevention, sharing our thoughts and feelings with our partner bolsters intimacy. Day-to-day frequent communication about our experience of our self and the world around us builds strong bonds. It provides the vigor needed to withstand the difficulties and storms of disagreement that inevitably blow our way.

Sharing deeply is not easy for many of us. There is a good deal of social conditioning to the contrary. Many of us have been inculcated with the cultural conviction that the less shared, the better. Men in particular have strong conditioning against communicating their feelings. The "strong silent type" is the model we have been raised to emulate. We believe that in order to be respected, we need to keep our feelings private. We do not share our inner challenges, but try silently to work out everything within. Yet it is precisely the sharing of our thoughts and feelings, the intimacies of our daily life, talking about the things that have hurt us, made us laugh, and embarrassed us, that brings us closer together. We come to "know" each other through these offerings. The definition of a stranger is someone we do not know. When we do not share ourselves with our partner, and they in turn do not share themselves with us, we remain strangers to each other.

The curative aspect of communication refers to the way in which it is an effective tool for resolving conflict once it has occurred. It is a way out of the dysfunctional and uncomfortable situations we create for ourselves as couples. It is particularly important when using communication to resolve conflict to first look for what is *right* in the other person's attitude, and to take responsibility for our part in creating the difficulty.

Our negative reactions and our subsequent, often mean-spirited communication to our partner generally arise because the other has touched a hurt place within us through their speech or behavior. We need to own our own feelings: that is, to take full responsibility for the fundamental fact that we are the ones experiencing our feelings. No one outside of ourselves can "make us" feel a certain way. Not blaming the other for the experience we are having inside of ourselves is the first and most important step on the road to skillful communication.

The alternative to reactive, unexamined, mean-spirited communication is, once again, *Going Vertical*. The skillful first movement when we have a strong reaction to our partner's behavior is to go within, to inquire what is happening in our own personal system, to examine the "vertical plane." We sense into what we are experiencing below the surface of our initial response in order to gain a deeper understanding of our reaction, rather than lashing out with hurtful speech or behavior as a result of being emotionally triggered. To work in this way we need to slow down our normally instant reactivity, and focus fully on experiencing our sensations instead of pushing them away because they are uncomfortable.

Once we have gained some insight into what is actually happening on the vertical plane, we are ready to move to the "horizontal plane," communicating our understanding to our partner. This style prevents the common mistake of engaging the mouth before the brain. Rather than a knee-jerk, fight-or-flight response, we can turn what might otherwise be an unpleasant conflict and painful estrangement into a moment of mutual understanding.

When I first began to teach about relationship I emphasized the importance of frequent, microscopic, in-the-moment communication. For instance, I believed that if Barbara put a glass of water on the table without a coaster and it bothered me, it was my solemn duty to say something immediately. Now, though I still believe it is important not to suppress my emotions and thereby create resentment in the long run, it is also important for me first to examine my own discomfort. Before I go immediately to the horizontal level and react to Barbara's behavior, telling her what is "right" and "wrong," I make a conscious effort to go vertical. Though saying, "Don't put the glass on the table—it stains," appears to be an honest and straightforward communication, by virtue of its inherently judgmental tenor, even if we do not mean it that way, it carries a tone of blame. Though my expression may solve my short-term problem about the table, it is likely to create distance between us. It is precisely the accumulation of this kind of petty communication that causes so much of the resentment and remoteness we see in long-term relationships.

Alternatively, I can slow down and go vertical. If I go within myself and sense what I am truly experiencing, something like the following statement might emerge: "Barb, that table is near and dear to me. The last time I put a wet glass on it, I was never able to get the ring out. I was really pissed off at myself for ruining it." Developing that vertical insight first, then communicating it, produces a better outcome. Before I begin spewing "my truth about you," which of course can only be conjecture, I need to examine the truth about me. A truth about me is something I have a chance to understand. My "truth about you" is generally superficial, reactive, and comes from an unexamined place within me.

A touching example of this skillful and connecting communication between a mother and her adult daughter is illustrative. Grace was very concerned about her daughter, Natalie. From Grace's perspective, Natalie was not managing her life well. Natalie had taken an extra semester to graduate from university, then stayed on campus an additional semester. When she returned home to live temporarily with her mother, Grace felt Natalie was not moving quickly enough towards a job and a place to live.

Grace bottled up these feelings as long as she could, but one Saturday evening they came tumbling out in an authoritarian parental rave. The incident caused a rift between mother and daughter. They did not speak to each other for days.

It was the daughter who first had the courage to go vertical and change the nature of the situation. After she had gained some insight into her own reactions, Natalie sat her mother down and said, "You know Mom, when you told me you think I can't manage my life, I felt hurt. It felt like you don't know me. You don't know who I really am. And that is a sore spot in me." Natalie's acknowledgment of her deeper truth brought forth Grace's inherent compassion for her daughter, and this sharing brought them closer together.

The next day, inspired by Natalie's example, Grace took the time to look at her own feelings. As she did, she began to feel very sad and started sobbing. As she stayed with her sadness, images of her other daughter, a young girl who had died many years before, arose in Grace's memory. The insight that she was transferring her feelings from that time and that young child to this time and this adult child became clear. Grace saw that she was afraid that given the way things were going, Natalie might not "survive."

Grace then took her turn to sit her daughter down and share this realization with her. Natalie was touched. She looked into her mother's eyes and without guile assured Grace that she could and would take care of herself. The daughter told the mother to rest assured, that she was capable of surviving and thriving in this world. Grace later told me that those words uttered under those conditions went in deep, and convinced her that Natalie could manage her life. Not only did their relationship improve, but Grace herself felt some further healing of the terrible loss she had experienced years before.

A more mundane, though typical example of this can be seen in my domestic life with Barbara. Previously, if she asked me twice in one day to "Please mow the lawn, it's getting higher than we like it," my superficial "truth" was expressed by saying with irritation, "You already told me about that." My deeper truth, however, which I can only recognize by taking my time, getting quiet, and going vertical, is "I'm overwhelmed right now. I can't handle even one more thing on my plate. I just need to zone out in front of the tube with some sports therapy." When I can find the strength first to go vertical, then the courage to go horizontal, communicating what I have learned through my inner examination, it will result in a mutually beneficial outcome. It produces understanding and connection rather than reactivity and anger.

I facilitated a session with a couple the other day, during which the woman was criticizing her husband for his habit of leaving their guests in order to take phone calls. I tried to help her go underneath this level of dissatisfaction and criticism of her mate and gain some insight into what was really going on for her. Sarah did not want to go there. She wanted to hold onto the moral high ground of her pleas for "good manners," and stay with the criticism. Like most of us, she was enjoying the satisfaction of being "right," and making her husband "wrong." With coaxing, however, she opened up and inquired into what was really going on. Checking in with herself, she noticed that the feelings she was experiencing when David left their guests to take a call was similar to the experience she had when he left her alone at the dinner table to answer the phone. They both worked all day, and with their busy lives dinner was the only quiet time they had together during the work week. His interrupting that time felt like a loss.

Having begun this inquiry, Sarah went further into her self and shared an even deeper level of insight She said that this sense of being shut off was reminiscent of the terrible feeling she had during an incident with her abusive ex-husband, who had stuffed a wad of paper into her mouth to shut her up. Upon hearing this, David felt a wave of empathy. As a way of supporting Sarah, he offered not to answer the phone at dinnertime, and to let the machine answer it when guests were present. This interchange resulted in increased self-awareness for Sarah, and a deeper understanding of Sarah by David. It brought them closer together, moving them in the opposite direction that Sarah's initial criticism had been taking them. When Sarah was complete with her process, and somewhat surprised by the outcome, she commented to me, "But don't all the relationship books say the most important thing is to ask for what you want?" My reply was, "Yes, and those books are Relationship 101, beginner's texts. We are more interested in the Senior Seminar. In mature relationship, we ask ourselves to stretch further, to go vertical before we go horizontal."

In another couples session, Ellie began to share with her husband Ricky that she didn't like what happened whenever his friend Norm came to visit. "You always end up chatting in some out-of-the-way corner, and when I approach the conversation stops. You're excluding me, and I wonder what kind of things you are talking about." This provoked a defensive denial from Ricky. The typical couples ping-pong match ensued: "I'm right, you're wrong." Fill in the blanks. It felt bad to both partners; a wedge was being driven between them with no resolution in sight.

I pointed out to Ellie that she was talking about her own feelings and trying to make Ricky responsible for them. She was trying to get Ricky to change his behavior so that she could feel better. This approach was a formula for disempowerment and frustration. If Ellie were to take responsibility for the fundamental fact that *she* is the one feeling excluded rather than seeing it as Ricky "making her" feel excluded, then the discussion could be fruitful rather than damaging. From an attitude of owning her feelings, Ellie would be poised to examine the real source of the experience of exclusion, which almost certainly runs deeper than this issue with Norm. Perhaps she would gain a measure of release from these uncomfortable feelings in the future.

When Ellie did choose to go within, she noticed that what she actually felt when Ricky was talking with Norm was an old and familiar sense of abandonment. At that point Ellie became quite emotional, and said, "This goes right back to my parents' divorce. I felt abandoned by my father then, and it has been a recurrent theme ever since." In that moment Ricky softened. He reached out to her, took her hand, and held her. He shared with her that he would like to do everything he can to help her feel comfortable and included, especially when Norm is around.

Having acknowledged the significance of first going inside before sharing with our mates, I would still like to emphasize the vital importance of eventually going horizontal. Going vertical is not enough to build intimacy. It is through sharing our self-awareness that understanding and closeness grow. Frequent microscopic communication between partners remains vital. Talking to each other a lot about everything, especially our personal thoughts and feelings, is critical. Offering even the small things we ourselves might deem unimportant goes far toward allowing us to appreciate each other and steer us clear of relationship potholes.

As we move more fully into owning our thoughts and feelings, and withdrawing our projections, we gradually become less prone to criticizing our partner, and more aware of who they and we truly are. When there is something that upsets us about our partner's behavior, and it is difficult to communicate for fear of hurting the other's feelings or starting a fight, I find that the communication model developed by Angeles Arrien is helpful. It offers a guide for how to communicate sensitive information while remaining authentic at the same time. It includes the vertical and horizontal planes. It calls for one to communicate what one *Sees*, *Feels*, *Wants*, and *Is Willing To Do*.

For example, if I am disturbed with Barbara for asking me too often to do a household chore (which is my responsibility that I am avoiding), before I reactively blurt in an unpleasant tone, "I'll get to it when I can," I first go inside to see what I am really experiencing. Once I can feel into it and get some clarity, I might say to her something like the following:

"Barb, *I SEE* that you have asked me a couple of times to change that light bulb."

"When that happens *I FEEL* like a little boy being told what to do by my mother."

"What *I WANT* is to be asked once, and to leave it at that."

"To satisfy your need that it gets done, what *I AM WILLING TO DO* is make a list of the sorts of things I can do for you around the house, and we can go over it every week to make sure we are on track."

When one uses this formula, the discussion proceeds from a context of full disclosure, and is more likely to result in a satisfactory outcome.

I saw a television show the other night in which one of the male characters was very angry at his girlfriend for falling asleep that night during their lovemaking—this because she was a medical intern who had worked the previous day for over 24 hours nonstop. Though comic in a certain way, it is easy to see how the situation would be upsetting to her boyfriend. Later, she was terribly embarrassed and repentant, and went to great lengths to explain her exhaustion and apologize. "It had absolutely nothing to do with you," she assured him repeatedly. "It was not what I wanted to do—my collapse was beyond my control." The man remained unmoved and angry for a long time.

As a viewer, I asked myself where his anger was really coming from. What was it being continuously fueled by? Sure, your girlfriend falling asleep on you is a real challenge to your manhood, but it never happened before, and was not typical of her sexual behavior; she was otherwise an enthusiastic lover. And, she apologized repeatedly. What more did this man need? Yet he continued to punish her with his anger. Given the imbalance between her attitude and his, the fuel to feed this rage must have been coming from somewhere else, from somewhere within him. This is a situation where the fellow needed to find the courage and integrity to withdraw his blame, examine himself, and try to understand where his reaction was coming from.

If the television character were to use the Angeles Arrien formula, he might say something like, "*I see* that you fell asleep while we were making love. That *feels* bad, and it really hurts my pride as a man. *I want* our love-making to be good for me and you. To help make that happen *I am willing* to let go of it when you are that tired." With this type of communication there can be conflict, followed by personal healing and interpersonal connection, even around difficult and sensitive issues.

Conversely, the fruit of non-communication is resentment. Not communicating about our self to our partner, not sharing our thoughts and feelings, particularly those that are generated in response to our partner, is colloquially called "stuffing it." Building up unspoken feelings, or "stuffing" them into the darkness of our psychic cellars, creates bitterness and animosity toward our partner. Resentment kills. Resentment and animosity create a negative filter through which we see our partner as flawed and against us. When our inner cellar can no longer hold the load of uncommunicated monsters we have created, we inevitably explode into mean-spirited speech or behavior. To make matters worse, such explosions are usually over an unrelated, irrelevant matter, and seldom over the real source of upset. Trying to resolve a conflict at the level on which it was created rarely provides a long-term solution. It may offer temporary relief, but inevitably the conflict returns. What is required is to go deeper, to the cause of the trigger—the wounds each partner has—and to speak from there.

There is a Sufi story that provides an analogy for this process. A man is looking for his keys under the streetlight, and a passerby asks him, "What are you dong?" "I am looking for my keys," the man replies. The passerby queries, "Did you lose them here?" "No," the man says, "but here is where I can see." We have to do better than that man. We have to go below the obvious, into the darkness, to the hidden but real sources of our losses to create harmony out of conflict.

A discussion at the level of the content of the argument without addressing the real source of upset will result in the continued ping-pong match of who is right and who is wrong, until one of the partners gets sufficiently frustrated to quit the scene physically or emotionally before resolution.

Resentment comes from pretending, from holding onto something that needs to be shared, yet acting as if we don't have to speak it because we feel safer that way. Some, in their desire not to pretend, their desire to be "honest," spew out unprocessed surface reactions that are hurtful to their partner, in the belief that they are doing the right thing because they are "speaking the truth." But what truth? What level of truth? How deep a truth? Our first rush of feelings in reaction to our partner is almost always at the unexamined superficial level. If we feel hurt, the conditioned first reaction is self-protective and often blaming. The thoughts accompanying this first reactive feeling are not the deepest "truth." Unexamined feelings and their associated thoughts are like unprocessed garbage: they quickly turn to stink. So, while we want to communicate frequently and honestly, it is vital that we first go vertical and see what is "truly" going on within us before we go horizontal and share our responses to our partner's words and deeds.

In a couples session, Seth and Erin spoke about one of their unfortunate moments of non-communication that resulted in a lot of pain for both of them. Erin had been told by her doctor that she needed a colonoscopy. This invasive medical procedure scared her, and she asked Seth to accompany her to the hospital for support. He agreed. A few days later, as they walked into the waiting area for the procedure, Erin felt Seth to be distant. This was different from his normally warm and supportive style. Seth didn't hold her hand or make any effort to comfort her. To Erin he seemed actually to be detached from her.

Subsequent to the procedure, and for many days afterward, Erin noticed that she was resentful towards Seth. Days turned into weeks, and though the initial reason for her discomfort with Seth was lost in memory, she found herself with a negative attitude towards him. She often felt judgmental of his behavior. This continued until one day when Seth, fed up with the cold shoulder, blew up at her. This fight, two steps away from the original cause of the conflict, irritated Erin even further, and became a major impediment in their relationship.

Two weeks later Seth broke a glass while he was doing the dishes. The irritating sound of the glass crashing, now three steps away from the original cause of the breach, blew Erin's fragile top. Seth, four steps away, then felt unjustly berated for an insignificant mishap. Hurt and confused, Seth withdrew into a shell, where he felt safe from Erin's judgment and anger, although it exacerbated the isolation and disconnection they both felt.

Finally the situation got so uncomfortable that it was no longer bearable. Erin decided to explore her own deeper feelings rather than continue to blame Seth for her discomfort. She rather quickly came to see that at the root of her feelings was the hurt of Seth's distance during the colonoscopy. She had felt unsupported and alone. Although she was ultimately given a clean bill of health, she felt abandoned when she needed Seth most. Erin summoned her courage to speak this to Seth, and finally told him her feelings with an effort to be free of judgment and blame. The waiting room incident, she said, felt reminiscent of her relationship with her dad, who was cold and distant, and seemed not to be there for her even when she was scared and needed him most. When the same feelings of abandonment arose around the colonoscopy, it upset her terribly.

In that moment Seth felt like a weight had been lifted from his shoulders. "Now I understand what is happening with you and where this is coming from. You weren't just being mean, you were hurt." With that understanding Seth felt he could be available to talk this through.

"I'm sorry you felt that way, Erin," he said. "But I was scared to death that you might be sick with something serious. I was so worried, I was doing everything I could to keep from breaking down so that I would be available to support you. I felt if I spoke to you, or even held your hand, I would collapse in tears and completely fall apart. I was doing the best I could to keep it together so I could be strong for you."

This interchange began clearing the logjam of resentment for them both. Erin saw what is a common miscommunication paradox between intimates: that her partner was actually trying to do just what she wanted, but that it was misunderstood. When Seth understood that Erin had not suddenly ceased to love him, things got much better for them as a couple. Only time will tell if, when the next challenge arises, they will employ their hard-earned communication lessons to extricate themselves from the distancing process. I hope so.

Though most problems between partners can be solved through responsible and honest communication, sexual difficulties represent one of the areas in a couple's life that is often difficult to effectively talk through and overcome. When the sexual connection is strained, it is often tough for partners to find their way back to a happy connection.

Barbara and I were experiencing just such problems some years ago. We were in the cliché dilemma of the man wanting more sex and the woman less, and experiencing the negative cycle this generates. One is "getting less," and so drives for more. The other is feeling "pushed," so fends off the partner even more vigorously. As each becomes more frustrated and hurt, they defend their own position more forcefully and attack the other's more assertively.

After some time it became clear to us that we were not going to get out of this negative cycle by ourselves. We decided to bring a fresh perspective into the equation by talking through the challenge in the presence of another couple with whom we felt comfortable and trusting.

They served as "fair witnesses," as neutral parties who helped create an atmosphere in which we both felt safer and more open. I spoke to Barbara about how bad it felt to be rejected in this intimate and vulnerable area of our lives. I explained that it felt humiliating trying to insinuate my way into sex. The sexual dilemma was getting in the way of feeling close with her in the other areas of our lives. Barbara spoke to me of feeling uncomfortably pressured to move at a pace that did not suit her. She said she needed to allow the sexual energy to arise more naturally, and not be forced. She needed things to go at a different pace than mine. She also said that she, too, was missing what had always been a beautiful and supportive part of our relationship.

Armed with this information, it became clear that we both needed to make some changes within ourselves and to learn to say "yes" to the other's needs. I needed to allow Barbara to lead the pacing of our sexual connection so she could feel open to me. She became aware of how important it was to find a way to have some kind of a "yes" response to my romantic advances without giving herself away when she didn't want to. This process helped us enormously. In the presence of fair witnesses, feeling safe enough to risk more vulnerable self-expression, we moved forward quickly. Soon our sexual connection returned to its previous fulfilling state, and allowed us to grow into an even more delightful sexual connection.

Another aspect of communication that is important in supporting healthy relationship is avoiding as much as possible the keeping of secrets. Secrets are too often deadly to intimacy. They have an insidious effect on both the person keeping the secret, and the one from whom the secret is being kept. Withholding information is like withholding part of oneself. It causes distance, first from our self, and then from our partner. It has a way of making our partner feel isolated from us.

On the other hand, sharing even what feels shameful frees one's energy and opens up the doors to understanding. This requires trust in our partner—sufficient trust to feel confident that we can share parts of ourselves we feel bad about, knowing that what we have shared will not be used against us as criticism or aggression. It requires trust that in return for sharing our vulnerability, we will get back understanding and support.

A powerful illustration of this, also related to sexuality, occurred in a group we were leading at Esalen Institute. For some months before the group began, I had been experiencing an intermittent level of sexual dysfunction—something I had never experienced before. It was extremely disturbing to me, and highly embarrassing. I was not open to talking about it with anyone. However, after a few days, a very safe atmosphere developed in this group, and I felt trusting of the people and secure in the circle. One of the exercises we asked people to do, precisely to demonstrate the power of not keeping secrets, was to share a secret.

When my turn came, I knew what I had to do. I felt myself get very anxious; my hands began to sweat and my body got hot. But, I had designed this exercise, and needed to model it with integrity. There was no better way than to speak what I really did not want to say. I blurted, "Sometimes I can't get a hard-on!" With those words released into the atmosphere, I expected to be annihilated, my world to collapse. What happened was just the opposite. I looked around, and not only was the earth unshaken, no one in the room was either. In fact, no one seemed to react very much at all. It was as if I had said, "We are having pancakes for breakfast." I felt a marvelous sense of relief. I had expressed a secret about which I had a lot of shame, a secret I felt I absolutely could not let out and still survive. I felt I would be harshly judged for my failure of masculinity. Yet nothing happened. No one thought less of me for having what I came to learn was a very common occurrence, one that most men experience at one time or another. Soon I felt free of the anxiety I was holding onto so tightly, trying to keep my secret. Interestingly, the physical problem itself faded away soon after. Apparently, the reduction in anxiety helped the energy flow again.

While the patriarchal style of non-communication produces neither meaningful connection nor peaceful relationships, the cocktail party style of superficial communication does not result in satisfying relationship either. Barbara and I continue to search for ways to break these culturally conditioned molds and go deeper with people. We have been only partially successful. As a result, we do not go to many gatherings where the cocktail party style of social interaction predominates. Nor do we any longer spend much time with people who are unwilling to share what is near and dear to their hearts. As a response to this challenge, we have developed and borrowed a series of evocative questions we use to drive conversation deeper. We use these questions to stimulate meaningful conversation between ourselves, occasionally with friends, and sometimes even with relatively new acquaintances, if they are amenable. Here are some examples:

- Do you know anything about the circumstances of your birth?

- Have you ever had a brush with death?

- Have you ever had a brush with the law?

- Have you ever been the recipient of injustice?

- What do you appreciate about yourself?

- What do you appreciate about me?

- What would you want me to know about you?

- What is your highest dream for your life?

- What were some of the peak experiences in your life?

- Who are your heroes?

- What were you like in high school?

- What do you remember about your first romantic relationship?

- Currently, what is the major challenge in your life?

- What were your grandparents like, and how has it affected who you are?

- What traumatic events in your life have in retrospect had a beneficial effect?

- As a child, what did you want to be when you grew up?

The couples therapist Susan Campbell has developed a game based on these sorts of penetrating questions. We sometimes use her questions with each other while we are driving in the car, or in a social situation where people are willing. In both cases it generates closer connection. It bonds people who have known each other for years, and those who hardly know each other at all. The power of evocative questions for those courageous enough to ask them, and for those courageous enough to answer them, is demonstrated by the following letter to *The Sun* magazine about a mother-daughter relationship:

"My mother and I are sitting on a beach in south Florida while my two sisters take a walk along the sand. In recent years, my relationship with my mother has improved to the point where I see her as another human being, rather than simply as a parent. Although our topics of conversation have always been superficial—sales, recipes, gossip—today, without really thinking about it, I ask whether she has any regrets in life.

She thinks for a moment and then says, very deliberately, "Yes, I regret having children." I am stunned. I wonder if this is a joke and wait for the punch line. As the day progresses, however, my heart starts to feel lighter. A contradiction that has puzzled me all my life is finally resolved. I've always had the sense that my parents didn't want us, and yet the thought seemed ridiculous. After all, they clothed, fed, and educated us. Now, thanks to my mother's revelation I can finally stop thinking I'm crazy. I feel strangely happy."[8]

Through a similar process, deep attachments are formed quickly between participants in personal growth workshops. We share our joy and pain in ways we are afraid to do in the everyday world. Revealing our strengths, weaknesses, and secrets connects us over the course of one weekend in ways that we sometimes cannot achieve with friends or family over a lifetime.

Barbara and I facilitate one couples group that has been meeting for over ten years. The connections both within and between the couples are profound at this point. All the personal and interpersonal work has opened windows onto one another's lives in ways that are very gratifying and supportive of intimacy. We have seen tremendous growth in the quality of the couples' relationships, and in the relationships between people in the group. The connection between partners has become more tender, and gratitude has become the predominant theme. Many obstacles to intimacy have been overcome, and couples have opened to the mutual kindness that marks superior relationships. In a quiet moment, as I sit back during a break in the group and look at these beautiful people while they are unaware of my gaze, I am so touched by what is possible for all of us in relationship. I see the manifestation of what I know is possible: joy, mutual compassion, and ultimately, peace.

Communication as both a preventative and healing tool goes far beyond the level of intimate relationship. It is the central and fundamental process of peacemaking at all levels: personal, interpersonal, and at the organizational, community, national, and international levels. Communication is the process through which differences can be settled without coercion and violence. It is a genuine alternative to war. War has been called a "failure of imagination." It might better be termed a "failure of communication."

Peace begins at the individual level. If each one of us commits to communicating well and fully, taking responsibility for our own feelings and speaking from that place, then there is no one blaming or being blamed. Then there is less reason to start or remain in conflict at any level, from the interpersonal to the international.

14 ⚹ U-Turn Only

Why do you see the speck that is in your brother's eye,
but do not notice the log that is in your own eye?
THE GOSPEL OF MATTHEW (7:3)

For the majority of us, the most troubling aspect of relationship is the conflict that arises between partners. Yet conflict between intimate partners is inevitable. We are each very different people with different habits and tendencies. If we are real, at some point along the way, either frequently or infrequently, conflict will arise. Like two boats moving forward on a parallel course, at some point our wakes will touch. At times they will merge in harmony, at other times they will clash in discord.

Both singles and couples attend the workshops we lead on intimate relationship. The singles often speak of yearning for a relationship. The couples often complain of the difficulties they have in relationship, and the pain of conflict they too often experience. Many of the couples express a longing for the peace of being single, and feel their lives would be easier alone. Acknowledging the inevitability of conflict and understanding its potential for healing and growth can reduce this frustration. Relationship is enhanced if we are conscious of our attitude toward conflict and respond to it with awareness. Conflict, if handled skillfully, can enhance intimacy.

Understanding the way in which each of us uniquely reacts in the presence of discord, no matter what its content, is an asset to handling conflict in a healthy way. Beyond the specific issue about which we are in opposition, what is our typical and general reaction in the face of friction? Do we run from it, fearing our associations with conflict and where it has led us in the past? Do we rush towards it, enjoying the excitement of battle? Do we stay with it, comfortably or uncomfortably, until we find resolution? If we are "conflict averse," it is useful to inquire into our feelings and commit ourselves to the Emotional Wisdom work that will allow us to "stay at the table" in the face of discord, until resolution emerges. Similarly, if our tendency is to rush into interpersonal battle, no matter what its content, it would be wise to understand what is at the core of this conditioning, then find a way to avoid engaging in conflict for its own sake. Knowing our tendency, and healing its dysfunctional aspects, allows us to bring less extraneous baggage into the conflict itself.

One couple I know, Noreen and Vern, have a terrible time when conflict arises because they are both so wounded around it. Though their disagreements do not rise to the level of physical violence, they do rise to such high levels of emotional heat that it is damaging to them as individuals and to their relationship. When I worked with Noreen and Vern, what became clear was that each of their chronic response patterns to interpersonal conflict was the key factor in creating their inability to process any specific disagreement.

As she went deeper, Noreen noticed that the feeling she experienced when she was in the presence of struggle was similar to one she felt in her family of origin. They continually fought about issues related to her disabled sister. Noreen felt what she described as a sour sensation accompanied by profound self-criticism. It was not okay to have her own feelings. She unconsciously believed that she should relegate herself to the background because her sister's needs had to take priority. When Noreen realized this, she understood for the first time that during conflict she was not seeing Vern as the man she loved, but as a surrogate sister who was stealing the family's love from her. These preconditions made it hard for Noreen to constructively engage in conflict. Fortunately, her insight into her history opened up the possibility for this to change.

Vern, for his part, noticed that his typical reaction to conflict was fear and the tendency to withdraw. He felt unloved in the presence of opposition. The feeling he associated with conflict was like the feeling he experienced in his family of origin, where fighting was the predominant mode of parental interaction. He was neglected and scared, and felt the only way he could be safe was to withdraw to his bedroom and stay out of the way. As happened with Noreen, Vern's insight into his own process offered him the possibility of alternatives. The ability to make more conscious choices enables a healthier process and offers more opportunity for constructive resolution.

There are many sources of conflict in relationship. Though we are intimate, each partner does not necessarily have the same standards, perspectives, and needs. These differences will, from time to time, come into opposition. The most important cause of discord in partnership is that we will not always get our own way. Our partner wants things to be a certain way too. They have an opinion, a need. The imperative is to find a skillful way to deal with this fundamental opposition.

The reason conflict goes beyond this initial and fundamental frustration, escalating to higher levels of intensity, is that something in the superficial opposition has touched an underlying and unhealed wound, an historically based emotional injury, as we saw in the case of Noreen and Vern, that often originates in our early life. The difference on the surface, the content of the disagreement, is rubbing on that tender place. Touching our raw spot causes a pain, and the tendency is to react with a fight-or-flight response, aggression, or withdrawal. In our effort not to feel our emotional pain, we allow the wounded aspects of ourselves to pass out of awareness. They then reside in our unconscious layer. As a result, we do not even realize that the wound has been touched. We just become hyper-reactive to the situation without awareness. The whole system contracts in response to the discomfort. We fall for the illusion that it is the content of our disagreement that is making us so uncomfortable. We are not even aware that it is actually the original emotional injury that has been activated.

As I have noted, in my case this process is triggered when someone "tells me what to do." If my partner, in the spirit of support, reminds me, "Did you take your checkbook with you?" as I go off to a doctor's appointment, I can easily take offense. Responding as if to a command, I feel reactive and may snap sharply in a mean-spirited way. But the truth is, if I slow down and become truly aware of my feelings, what I realize is that my childhood wound around being controlled has been activated. It is blinding me to the simple reality of the present, and I respond as if in a time machine to the past.

The way out of conflict and into personal growth and healing in relationship is through diminishing judgment and blame, and owning our feelings. We need to possess as our own the discomfort we feel while in conflict with our partner. It is *our* feeling in *our* body. It may be triggered by the other, but the actual sensation of discomfort lies within us. The best way to respond to this reality, the most empowering way, is to withdraw our focus from the other and the differences between us, and concentrate our attention within, on the feelings and teachings lodged inside the discomfort. Going into the feeling and drawing down the wisdom hidden in the emotion allows insight to emerge. Sometimes it even allows release from the limitations imposed by the feelings. Understanding this, we can shift our beliefs about conflict from seeing it as a wholly negative experience to a positive, if difficult, one.

The process of owning our projections we call the *U-Turn*. And the best way to deal with the feelings that arise in conflict we call *U-Turn Only*. The heightened feelings that generate conflict, which we have been discussing throughout this book, are fundamentally projections. We are seeing a disowned part of our self in the other. When we begin to point the finger at the other as wrong, the more skillful response is to make a gentle U-Turn: that is, to kindly turn the interest and inquiry back to ourselves, lightly beginning a loving self-investigation. What within us has been triggered?

Again using my own unhealed wound as an example, if Barbara advises me that my shirt is dirty and I should probably change it, I can easily get angry and make her wrong for telling me what to do. However, if I make a U-Turn, using my awareness of the discomfort arising within me as a reminder to go deeper and inspect myself, what I notice is that the real energy in my reaction comes from a very crusty old feeling of aversion to what I perceive as control. As I stay with the inquiry, feeling into my own feelings, I can recall when I first began to have these feelings—as a disempowered child constantly controlled by adults and relatively powerless to get my own way.

As I come to understand the origin of this complex, I also understand that those conditions no longer exist. I am no longer a disempowered child. I am a fully empowered adult. I do not need to react from a disempowered place anymore. I can choose to change my shirt or choose not to change my shirt, free of any conditioned reactivity. The insight brings me clear vision. My partner just made a suggestion. I can take it or leave it. By making the U-Turn, I advance my healing, freeing myself a bit more from this particular box. The next time it happens, I hope to respond more in the present than from the past, acting with more grace, whatever shirt I wear.

The U-Turn is the first step in the process of Going Vertical and then Going Horizontal. By inquiring within and then communicating about our self to the other rather than communicating about how the other is wrong, conflict is minimized and resolved. Now, instead of attacking, we are sharing about our self. Attacking creates distance and aversion. Sharing creates intimacy.

The process of reacting to our partner, noticing our reactivity, then making the U-Turn is, for better or worse, a never-ending enterprise. Because of our deep conditioning, how we adapted emotionally and physically to survive the war zone of childhood, there is always another layer that appears after the previous layer has been removed. That should not deter us. It is the best game in town. As in dropping physical weight, the lighter we get, the more easily we move. We become more graceful, we handle the challenges more skillfully, and we feel better.

Owning our projections is the anvil upon which the growth process is hammered out. If we are willing to do the self-work, we will come to deeply appreciate the immense value for personal growth that intimate relationship offers. Robert Johnson, in *Owning Your Own Shadow*, illustrates how taking responsibility for our projections in relationship can be playful as well as helpful. He writes, "I recently heard about a couple who had the good sense to call upon the shadow in their wedding ceremony. The night before their marriage, they held a ritual where they made their 'shadow vows.' The groom said 'I will give you an identity and make the world see you as an extension of myself.' The bride replied, 'I will be compliant and sweet, but underneath I will have the control.' They then drank champagne and laughed heartily at their foibles, knowing that in the course of the marriage, these shadow figures would inevitably come out. They were ahead of the game because they had recognized the shadow and unmasked it."[9]

A stunning example of our blindness to our inner process is the case of the professional athlete who pretended to have such a strong Christian morality that he refused to visit the White House after his team's Super Bowl victory because President Clinton was "immoral." He was soon after accused by his 17-year-old babysitter of getting her drunk and forcing sex upon her on the bathroom floor just after her return from the Catholic High School prom. Consider also the Moral Majority leader who, after damning homosexuals to hell, was caught in a homosexual affair with a male prostitute.

A less graphic, but still relevant example is the case of Bill and Joanne, who came to me for couples work. They explained that they existed in an almost constant state of battle. Bill said, "I don't trust Joanne. I can't trust what she says or does."Upon making the U-Turn, it became clear to Bill that because of his own personal history and some mistakes he had made in the past, the person he really didn't trust was himself. He projected that distrust onto his wife. He was seeing himself in the mirror of his intimate partner.

Joanne said that Bill did not "accept" her. He didn't listen to her or "receive" her. She also said that Bill was constantly judging her. When Joanne made her U-Turn and examined the feelings associated with this story, she saw that she was primarily the one who did not accept herself. Her habit, stemming from a critical father, was to judge herself constantly and harshly. Joanne was seeing this reflected in the mirror of her intimate partner.

By the end of our work together, Joanne understood and acknowledged this truth about herself. Because of that, she experienced some healing and peace. Bill recognized that the source of his reactivity was not Joanne. That resulted in Bill being less judgmental of Joanne and more at ease with himself in the relationship.

Herman Hesse, the brilliant German novelist, wrote, "Whenever we hate someone, we are hating some part of ourselves that we see in that person. We don't get worked up about anything that is not in ourselves." The crazy truth is, it really is "all about me." After we had hammered this point home for two days at a workshop in England, one participant saw the humor in it all and said to me at the end, "I was going to tell you that you are gifted and talented at this work, but now I know that it's just a projection, and *I* am the one who is gifted and talented."

Another frequent cause of interpersonal conflict in relationship, and the fuel that feeds its fire, is the need to be right. Many arguments are not so much about the subject in dispute as about two people fighting to be right. More often than fighting to be right, we are really fighting not to be wrong. This, like many of the dynamics discussed here, is most often a result of early experiences in which being right was safe, and being wrong was unsafe. If you gave the "right" reply to your father, mother, schoolteacher, or other authority figure in your early life, you might avoid a negative or punitive response. In the present, as an adult, that conditioning remains. When in conflict, there is a part of us that is desperately trying to avoid being wrong, because at the unconscious level being wrong is associated with the potential pain of punishment. So we fight to be right.

When Barbara and I finally realized how often the fuel at the bottom of our conflicts was the struggle to be right, we instituted a simple, humorous, but highly effective solution. Having become aware that most of our arguments were over trivial matters and mainly a struggle not to be wrong, we decided on an automatic solution. We divided the days of the week equally into those days in which Barbara was by fiat defined as "right," and those in which I was "right." On Monday, Wednesday, and Friday, Howard Joel was right. On Tuesday, Thursday, and Saturday Barbara was right. On Sunday we would just duke it out. Though seemingly nonsensical, this method helped enormously. It made us keenly aware of how the actual content of our conflicts did not really matter, but was an attempt to stay safe in the face of disagreement. The safety provided by the formality and equality of this process proved to us that we can easily drop our need to be right, and that doing so is unlikely to cause harm. It helped raise our consciousness about the nature of conflict, safety, being right, and being wrong. Now we no longer need this structure. It has dropped away like the boosters on a rocket. We seldom argue over trivial matters anymore.

Along with the wish to be right is the innate desire to be heard. There appears to be some deep-seated need within us to be received and acknowledged. It seems to parallel the experience of the infant who comes to know herself by seeing herself reflected back by the adults around her. Being heard allows us to feel that we exist and matter. I get very frustrated if Barbara does not respond to what I have said in a way that indicates she has heard me. I need an acknowledgment that she has listened and tried to understand what I am saying in order for me to relax and listen well to her. If this does not happen, my attention is tied up in pushing my way into being understood, and not on listening to Barbara.

Our friend Kate had the same issue, expressed in a somewhat different way, with her husband John. For me, feeling that I have been heard is getting a sense that my partner has listened and tried to understand me. For Kate, it was seeing action forthcoming based on what she had said. When John did not follow through on her requests to him, she felt she had not been heard. If Kate asked John to slow down while driving and John acknowledged her request, but eventually began to speed up again, or when she asked him to do something around the house and he said he would, but never got around to it, then she felt unheard, misunderstood, and frustrated. This caused Kate to build up a weighty bag of resentment toward, and distance from, John. She began to feel closed off to him as well. Eventually it reached into the bedroom, and Kate was no longer receptive to lovemaking. She literally felt she could not be open and receiving to someone who was not open and receiving to her. It was this issue of being heard that had to be worked through before their sexual life, and ultimately their intimacy, could be restored.

15 ❧ From Counterclockwise to Clockwise

*C*hronic conflicts tend to emerge out of issues in which the same content triggers different wounds in each person at the same time. It is the classic double-edged sword. Both are cut by the same sword, each by a different side of the blade. Both sides of the blade cut, but each side cuts into different flesh. This is confusing and makes resolution difficult. It requires both partners to be conscious and choose to experience the source of their own reactivity while simultaneously maintaining a supportive attitude toward the other.

We have often seen that issues having the character of a double-edged sword generate conflict that, once it has begun, spins out of control and takes on a life of its own. The conflict seems to spin deeper and deeper in a seemingly hopeless direction, what I call a *counterclockwise* direction. Each move by each partner turns the wheel of resolution and satisfaction in a negative, unsatisfactory, counterclockwise direction.

For instance, Marcia tells Jimmy, "I need more space." Upon hearing this Jimmy has a strong reaction. He is angry and feels unfairly pushed away. Actually, he is re-experiencing an early pattern of emotional abandonment by his parents, but is not aware of it. Jimmy tries to get closer to Marcia in an effort to diminish the discomfort he is feeling. This behavior, of course, triggers Marcia to feel even more invaded. She tries to take more space by moving even farther away emotionally. The double-edged sword here is pushing the wheel in a counterclockwise direction.

The challenge then is to turn that wheel in the opposite direction, to get the spin going in a positive, clockwise, relationship-building direction.

The way, of course, is through our often-emphasized method of each partner Going Vertical and then Horizontal: discovering what is motivating our own personal stuckness and communicating that insight to the other.

So, Mary needs to say more than, "I want more space." She needs to own that the feeling of not having enough space is hers, without blaming or making it about Jimmy. She might say something like, "When we get so close I feel uncomfortable. It reminds me of the feelings I had with my father, who always seemed to be smothering me." Jimmy, for his part, needs to go beyond the "you" statement of "I feel you are abandoning me," and change it to something like, "When I hear you ask for more space it feels just like what my last girlfriend said before she left me for another guy." This puts both partners in an understanding rather than an adversarial position. This is the kind of communication that will turn an issue from spinning in the counterclockwise direction towards positive, clockwise movement.

The distinction between going deeper to resolve conflict and staying stuck on the surface spinning was apparent in the difference between two couples I worked with during the same period: Lana and Ed, versus Melanie and Burke.

Ed was fixed on how Lana did not want to have enough sex. No matter how hard we tried to get Ed to go below the surface to see what he was really feeling, he was not willing to make himself vulnerable enough to do that. As a result, though Lana explored the deeper reasons for her lessening interest in sex with Ed, the counterclockwise cycle was never broken. In the two years I worked with them, the sexual connection did not improve, and the quality of the relationship stagnated as well.

In stark contrast was the process of Melanie and Burke. In the beginning Burke was adamant and angry that Melanie was not sufficiently committed to him and the relationship. No matter what Melanie said or did, no matter how she explained herself, or how deep she went, Burke was not satisfied. He remained angry and convinced that Melanie was not committed. Then, during a session in which I suggested that he feel deeply into the sense he gets when he experiences Melanie as not committed, Burke had an insightful experience. He saw that the real issue was not that Melanie was not fully committed, but that *he* was not fully committed. He wanted to be, he pushed himself to be, he acted like he was, but underneath he had a big question mark about his own commitment. In two of his previous committed relationships he had been hurt. With that realization, over time Burke naturally withdrew the pressure for Melanie to be different, and focused instead on his own wound-generated doubt. When Burke no longer defined Melanie as not sufficiently committed, Melanie felt free to behave in ways that in fact felt more committed to Burke. The process turned out elegantly, and things between them improved substantially.

Again, it is good to be reminded that conflict is not all bad. If handled skillfully, the couple will grow from it, coming out wiser and at a new level together. If we hold a bigger perspective while working our way out of a stuck place, knowing that it is a potential growth point for the relationship, then the whole matter can be experienced more lightly and with some level of humor for the human condition. Hold a good attitude toward stuckness. It comes about because we are up against something in ourselves that we are ready to heal. It is arising to be healed, and that is a gift.

Conflict between partners is difficult not just because the discord itself is so unpleasant, but because the feelings associated with it carry such an unconscious charge. When there is ongoing and chronic conflict about a matter, it is fair to assume that the underlying cause of the conflict is not being addressed. We are stuck on the surface where the true cause does not reside. Logic, when dealing with conflict in couples, especially the double-edged sword variety, is more than useless. Staying with the logical arguments about who is right regarding the content of the dispute will not resolve the conflict; it will only drive it in deeper. Logic does not address the true source of the reactions, and therefore will not produce a true and lasting solution.

All of us are familiar with the frustration of logically arguing with our partner and getting absolutely nowhere. They logically argue back, making their case, and we too remain unmoved. Each of us presses on with increasing energy, looking for the rational counterpoint that will prove we are "right." But this is impossible. Neither the energy propelling us to be "right," nor the source of our reactions, has anything to do with logic. Both are entirely outside the logical realm, hidden below the surface, and impervious to reason.

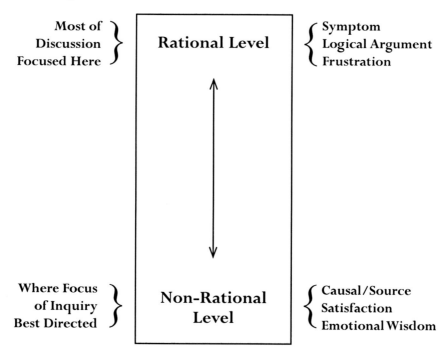

With this understanding Jane Addams, the famous social activist and founder of the Settlement House movement of the early 20th century, noted that "all conflict is false." What she meant by that seemingly unreasonable statement is that opposition, at the level we experience it, is not real. The conflict is just a marker on the surface for the source that lies below. Just as we are called to go beneath the apparent conflict, we also have the possibility of going "above" it to find resolution. To go above it means to connect with ourselves at the spiritual level, where there is no real opposition. From these heights we have enormous perspective, and can easily see the triviality of almost all interpersonal conflict.

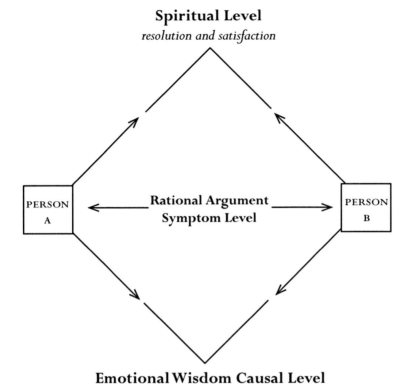

Spiritual Level
resolution and satisfaction

PERSON
A

**Rational Argument
Symptom Level**

PERSON
B

Emotional Wisdom Causal Level
resolution and satisfaction

A double-edged sword in my life is the one I have already discussed: issues that trigger a sense of not being heard. When I feel misunderstood, I can easily get reactive and angry, and raise my voice. Barb's side of that sword is her fear of anger. Her life experiences have taught her that anger is often followed by danger. Though she would like to listen and understand me, when I am angry it is difficult for her to make the choice to do so. She is caught in this negative conditioning. We are both pierced on different sides by the same sword.

The way out is either down or up. Recognizing this, we see that conflict resolution is often conflict dissolution; we dissolve rather than resolve the difference. We extinguish the conflict by removing the fuel that feeds it. In this way we learn to live the maxim, "antagonism is a temporary stage in the movement towards common ground."

16 ✤ Conflict Resolution

*T*here are numerous techniques for conflict resolution. The following have been successful for Barbara and me, as well as for many of the couples we have worked with.

A powerful approach, discussed previously, is something we call *Dropping the Bag*. Each of us has a bag full of issues. These bags are filled with the emotional refuse accumulated over a lifetime. We carry these bags with us as "excess weight" luggage in the present. As we have mentioned, the most challenging conflicts are the double-edged swords, in which the issue or behavior in question has historical roots, and is present in both our bags.

As a way of out of these difficulties, one partner can consciously and voluntarily choose to drop their bag. One partner recognizes that they are in reactivity, and chooses to temporarily abandon their attachment to the triggered state and become a listener. We stop trying to force the other to understand us, and instead remain present for them.

To drive the process deeper and help one get into a new, more positive habit, it is helpful to literally embody the process. Each person gets a small brown bag, takes a tissue and gives it the name of the reactive place it represents, then physically puts it into the bag. While each holds their bag full of unprocessed historical material, one partner volunteers to literally drop their bag on the floor and listen. The listener then becomes a restorative agent rather than an antagonist. In many ways this approach imitates the therapeutic process, in which one person works on their emotional material while the other holds a non-reactive, supportive stance.

A great deal of healing and growth comes through this approach to conflict resolution. And the next time a flare-up on this level arises, the other partner can take their turn, drop their bag, and be the empathetic listener. This is the epitome of the Healing Relationship.

Another effective way to resolve conflict is to symbolically move the locus of conflict from between the two people, putting it in front of both. This act shifts the behavior of the partners from conflict to mutual problem-solving. Now, instead of a bone we are haggling over, we have a problem in front of us that we need to solve cooperatively. Ordinarily, the physical arrangement in conflict involves two people facing one another, struggling over the issue that stands between them. In this new scenario, the partners arrange themselves shoulder to shoulder, putting the problem in front of them rather than between them. The challenge is to solve the problem together. In this way the conflict turns from a fight to be right at the expense of the other, into an exercise of team-building through problem-solving.

To help make this shift you can put an actual object between you, like a tissue box, letting it represent the matter in dispute. Then physically move yourself shoulder-to-shoulder with your partner, and the object from its position between you to a position in front of you. This is the problem-solving position. This physical embodiment, representing a new and team-oriented approach, is often surprisingly helpful.

Yet another way to shift struggle into learning is to stand facing each other at some distance and to begin the discussion around the dispute. Each person, upon hearing what their partner says, represents how that statement makes them feel by moving toward their partner when it feels good, or away from them when it feels bad. The distance between partners is a measure of how each feels based upon the nature of their partner's communication during the dispute. By working with conflict in this way, each partner gets immediate feedback on how their speech, body language, and attitude affect the other. They can see how it impacts the closeness and intimacy of their relationship and how they themselves respond to the other's style. It is enlightening and, when undertaken with goodwill, can be very helpful in understanding how to be in conflict in a way that generates intimacy.

A further helpful way to resolve chronic conflict is to invite a "fair witness" into the process. A fair witness is a trusted, impartial third party. This brings an element of safety into the dispute, which allows for deeper and more helpful communication. It creates an atmosphere that feels more secure and makes it is easier to speak truth from the heart, and also to listen more sympathetically to the other. With a fair witness, a more positive context for conflict resolution is possible. Each partner tends to act with more consideration and kindness toward the other in the presence of a third party, and to work more for resolution than to be right or win. The fair witness need not be a professional, or trained in therapeutic skills—simply a person with integrity whom both partners trust to be fair, a person who is not afraid of conflict, can witness the dialog around it, and can occasionally offer a helpful insight.

It is important to find effective approaches to conflict resolution that work for your relationship, because without a clear atmosphere between partners, resentment builds and intimacy declines. Resentment is, for the most part, pent-up anger. It needs to be discharged in a healthy way so that it does not damage us, our partner, or the relationship. In one way or another it is critical that you proceed without judgment or blame, first Going Vertical within yourself, then sharing with the other what is going on with you, with no expectation that they must change to accommodate you.

Sometimes we are so caught up in our fear of confrontation that when we do address a problem with our mate, rather than doing it in a loving way, we unconsciously make them the enemy in order to get up the nerve to face them. As an alternative, when the time comes that you feel you must confront your partner to maintain your own self-respect, keep your heart open to them while doing so. You don't need to close your heart to speak your truth. You can stand for yourself without making the other wrong. Conflict is most easily resolved when you hold love in your heart while speaking your own truth.

Even understanding this, it is valuable to remember that conflict resolution—whatever the methods, techniques, or attitudes we take to it—is often not a process of short duration. Consequently, it is helpful to "stay at the table" until the conflict is resolved. "Conflict resolution interruptus" can create more harm than good. Resolution not arising as quickly as we would like is not a reason to run from it. We need to stay with the conflict resolution process all the way to clarity. That does not mean we can't call time out or take a break from the heat of the process, but that we keep coming back to the table until there is clear space between us.

Trust is key in helping to resolve conflict between partners. We need to know that the other is fundamentally on our side in order to be vulnerable in their presence. To reveal our inner process, the information we mine when we Go Vertical requires a belief that this material will not be used against us, and that we do not have to fear emotional reprisal. Without trust, resolution of differences is difficult. It is crucial in intimate relationship to do all we can to build and maintain trust. We need to "do what we say, and say what we do." We need to be honest and follow through on our word. Not just in order to occupy the moral high ground, but for the sake of the quality of our relationship.

When trust is broken, it is difficult to repair. Though hard to mend, it is vital that we make every effort to do so. The behavior or words that broke the trust need to be sincerely examined, both individually and together. We each need to take responsibility for our part in the trust-breaking experience, and find the capacity to forgive our self and the other. If forgiveness is not present, if trust is not rebuilt, conflict will be more frequent due to the presence of resentment. Resolution will be more difficult because each event carries a piece of the trust-breaking experience into it, and intimacy in general will be hard to find.

Some of us have a hard time "letting go" and forgiving the other for what we feel is a transgression of trust. Yet, we are all human. We all, every single one of us, make mistakes. We are all as capable of missteps as our partner. If we can see the fallibility in our self, be gentle, accepting, and forgiving of our self, then perhaps we can forgive our partner when they violate the faith we have placed in them.

As we have said, conflict can be destructive or constructive, depending on how we approach it. It offers a significant opportunity for growth and healing. Nancy Steinbeck, John Steinbeck's wife, in her book about her life with her famous author husband, wrote: "Fortunately, when a bond is strong, when two souls are seamless, the real healing of childhood wounds can take place. John's drunken excess held a mirror to my enabling code-pendency and my outrage reflected his craziness back to him. That simple act became our salvation. Although the journey was often ghastly, it served us well."[10]

17 ❦ Sex

Sexual love is the most stupendous fact of the universe,
and the most magical mystery our poor blind senses know.
AMY LOWELL

Sex is generally trouble-free and fulfilling in the beginning of a relationship, thanks to the power of lust. Yet for many couples sexual fulfillment deteriorates over time. After a time, and with familiarity, sheer lust diminishes, and on its own is not enough to sustain a gratifying sexual relationship. After unsuccessfully struggling with this devolution, many couples despair and assume that their sexual connection will no longer be enjoyable. They give up or seek excitement outside of the relationship. It does not have to be this way. It can be different. Sex can get even better as the relationship grows. We can move forward from the strictly lustful stage, to a stage of mature, passionate sexual union.

Sex, besides all its other magical qualities, is a form of communication. If the other communication channels between partners are open and healthy, it is highly likely that the sexual channel will also be open and healthy.

In the beginning, sexuality is generally male-oriented. It follows our cultural image of "hot sex," as portrayed and promoted through the media: "doing the wild thing," assertive, hard-charging, even aggressive. The image of a macho man clearing the kitchen table and throwing his woman on it for sex, or passionately pressing her against the wall and taking her. That kind of sex is great. It's exciting, it's fun, and it feels wonderful. But it is not the kind of sex that endures. It is the 100-yard dash, not the marathon of a long-term relationship. It is not sustainable over distance. Still, many hold this image of sexual connection as how it should always be. If it is not, then the sex does not measure up, and either I or my partner is a failure.

Much of the problem in the perceived diminishment of the quality of sexual contact comes from couples comparing what they have against this perceived cultural standard, and judging theirs as "less than." The effort to squeeze into a form that does not fit, that is not authentic for where a couple naturally is, and where they are evolving to over time, can turn into a vicious judgmental cycle. What does work is to think of the process as one of evolving from a male model of sexuality—which in reality is adolescent male sexuality—to a more mature form. We can call it female-centered sexuality. It is a model that is gentler, slower, and more round than arrow-like in nature. Yet it is every bit as passionate—perhaps in the long run even more satisfying, because it involves a deeper form of communication, and is not only physically pleasing, but also builds genuine connection.

As it is the female who must energetically and physically open to the male for sexual union, it is appropriate that it follow her propensities and lead. What this generally means is more talk, a longer period of connecting verbally and energetically, and allowing the aliveness to arise naturally before physical sex is initiated. Moving from the Hollywood assumption that all that is necessary for good sex is the desire to be sexual, and that our partner will automatically pick up on our desire, to a relationship based on open and honest communication, is the beginning of satisfying, mature sexual union. The feminine communication model of sex is linking verbally, and nurturing a melting, flowing sexuality, waiting for the energy to arise naturally.

Once during a workshop, a couple was having a disagreement about a fence they were building in their backyard. The man wanted one design, and the woman another. They were making very little progress on the fence. Another participant in the group spoke up and said, "What you have to understand is you are not building a fence. You're doing a project together. It is about the doing together that is the most important part. Not the fence." We all were hushed, and saw the truth in that insight immediately. This wisdom applies to sex as well. It is a cooperative project. It is not something to be accomplished the way I want it, or you want it. It is not something to be measured against a vision of mine or yours. It is designed to connect us through mutual pleasure. If it does not do that, then it has not served its true purpose. What the fence actually looks like, what the sex actually looks like, is secondary. It certainly does not have to look like the cultural norm, or what the newlyweds are up to down the street.

Mature sex is not about giving up passion. It is not about giving up pleasure. It is not about settling for less. Quite the opposite. When the sex is working for both partners, the passion flows freely. When the process fits the people rather than trying to fit the people to an image, the sex is great.

In the feminine model, which emphasizes sex as communication, if what is required of the woman is to open physically, then what is required of the man is to open emotionally. The latter facilitates the former. In the numerous couples I have worked with, a constant complaint I hear from the man is that his woman is not open to having sex as often as he would like. Yet often those very same men seem blind to the fact that they are not open to the woman's emotions.

In the case of Janice and Jim, he was vociferous about "this problem my wife has." When I asked Janice her view, she said, "Truly, deep down, I feel like I hardly know him. He rarely talks about how he feels." So, Janice did not feel safe enough emotionally to open physically to someone so distant and unknown. How could she make herself so utterly vulnerable to someone who is an emotional stranger? Janice and Jim were making very little progress on this problem. No matter how often I pointed out the logic to Jim, he steadfastly refused to take it in. The cultural image had him literally by the balls. His unexamined core belief was that men don't talk about their feelings, and sex looks like what he used to have with his girlfriends in college. Yet in the present, Janice balked and Jim was frustrated. The clash was spilling over into almost every aspect of their lives, making their companionship and family atmosphere very unpleasant.

The quality of the sexual relationship in a couple is generally a reflection of the quality of the relationship itself. It is symptomatic of the emotional health of the bond in all its complexity, manifested in physical form. If there is open communication between the partners, if there is cooperation, if there is equality, if resentment does not build, if there is trust and safety, then the sexual connection will naturally flow into fulfilling mature sexual love. If these elements are not present, if open communication is absent, if the relationship is stagnant and not a form through which both partners are growing, then it is likely the sexual connection will grow fallow and move in a counterclockwise direction. Consequently, it is seldom skillful to seek solutions to sexual dissatisfaction in the purely mechanical or physical realm. New positions and unusual physical arrangements can be fun and provide diversion, but they are not likely to turn the cycle in the clockwise direction. What will help is to find where in the overall relationship there is a problem, and then address it. If the emotional problem is healed, the sexual connection will follow.

Because sex is so much about communication, it is often the case that a couple experiencing sexual problems is also experiencing a lack of verbal intimacy, a lack of sharing their inner reality, talking about their challenges and joys with one another. This kind of verbal sharing creates intimacy and a sense of safety, which allows openness and abandon to the beauty of sexual love. The way out of chronic sexual problems and into rekindling the sexual fire is through the emotional healing work described in the chapter on Emotional Wisdom. This means doing the U-Turn, taking the blame off our partner and Going Vertically into the feelings associated with our own sexual frustration, then sharing that information with our partner verbally. This approach is likely to result in an improved sexual connection.

For many people, sexual dysfunction emanates from childhood sexual abuse. For those who have been victims, the experience can create a significant block in their adult sexual functioning. Sharing the story with our partners can help, but deeper psychological work is often needed to heal and become a fully open sexual being. With the help of an experienced guide, going into the pain of the abuse and releasing some of the trapped feelings can open up wonderful possibilities.

Janet, a beautiful woman of about 35, was having a lot of conflict with her boyfriend around their sexual intimacy. He complained it was not frequent enough. She complained he was constantly pressuring her. They went around battling in this counterclockwise circle, getting more and more frustrated. After working with Janet and Jim for a number of sessions, I decided to do a few sessions with Janet on her own, focusing on the sexual abuse she had experienced as a child. Janet's grandfather, a fundamentalist minister, had been the perpetrator. He would come to her bed in the evening, force sex upon her, then leave after admonishing Janet never to tell anyone, or she would "burn in hell." Believing him, she remained silent and trapped in an emotional corner until her mid-20s, when she first shared this history with a friend.

Upon hearing the story myself, and being with Janet's tears, I asked her to check in even more deeply with the sadness she was presently feeling. With this, she felt a pain in her pelvis. Then images of the encounters with her grandfather in her childhood bedroom arose. Janet stayed with her discomfort, and the images and the pain intensified. Then, quite suddenly, she emitted a big exhale and groan, almost a shriek. In that moment she experienced the sensation of great physical release, accompanied by the spontaneous onset of her period. Simultaneously, an insight arose in her in the form of words, and she blurted out, "It's time to let go and move on." This is a dramatic example of what is usually a longer and slower process. Through doing the Emotional Wisdom Work around her sexual issues, Janet gained a greater sense of freedom and optimism about the future.

Marie was having similar issues. She was disinterested in sex, and had frequent struggles with her husband about his dissatisfaction. When she and I explored the issue more deeply, Marie felt the chronic hip pain she had been experiencing, seemingly over a lifetime, begin to well up. When she dove into it, a specific memory of a period in her 20s arose, when Marie contracted herpes from her college boyfriend. The experience left her ashamed and judging herself as promiscuous. When she entered into a dialog with the discomfort in her hip, what she heard was, "I want you to be pure." I then asked her to ask the hip, "Tell me more about wanting to be pure." What she got in return was, "Forgive yourself. You are pure." With those words she felt a lightening, a diminishment of the discomfort in her hip, and sexual energy coursing through her. I have seen Marie in follow-up sessions, and in her words she is "sexually renewed."

When a couple gets into chronic sexual difficulty, it is as if they are in a spider web. The more they struggle with it at the superficial level, the more entangled they become. This was true for Bill and Liz. Bill was making every effort to be honest and real in expressing his frustration with not having frequent enough sex with Liz. Upon hearing that, Liz felt extremely pressured. Every time she heard this complaint, which was Bill's honest and frequent expression of his feelings, Liz felt an even heavier weight of demand. In response, she withdrew more.

I asked Liz to really feel into this sensation she called "pressure," and to physically act it out. She got up and slowly started to move backwards, constricting her body, until she literally backed herself into a corner and bent over into a totally closed, defensive position. I asked her what she was feeling in that corner, in that stance, and she said, "This feels like my relationship with my older brother, Teddy." Then I checked in with Bill, inquiring into his frustration. Bill's fundamental sentiment was, "I feel like I can never win." Inspecting that feeling further, it became clear to Bill that this was lifelong baggage, rooted in his family of origin. His authoritarian parents made him feel that nothing he ever did was right.

The sexual dynamics between Bill and Liz were coming from a completely different source then their own bedroom; they were coming from the homes they grew up in. Yet in struggling without this insight, each trying to be right and safe, they exacerbated the problem. Without working at the Emotional Wisdom level, things just got worse and worse.

As a healing intervention I had Bill and Liz reverse roles. I led Bill into the corner, asked him to take the physical stance Liz had been holding, and feel into that discomfort. Bill squirmed and felt tears well up. I then asked Liz to talk Bill out of his corner, a symbolic representation of Bill trying to talk Liz into sex. The result was Bill wedging himself further into the corner. Liz could now feel the frustration of the powerlessness Bill had been experiencing with her. This was the first time each felt understood by the other, and had insight into what was really going on between them. From complete despair they moved to a feeling of possibility. Now they were in a good position to turn the wheel from counterclockwise to clockwise. At a minimum, they were not digging themselves in deeper, and had more compassion and mutual understanding.

When the sexual cycle is stuck or moving in the wrong direction, what is needed is a change in the nature of the conversation. What is needed is a move from "I don't get enough" on one side, and "don't pressure me" on the other, to "what is going on underneath this feeling for me?" and "what is going on underneath this feeling for you?"

The problem Bill and Liz experienced in sex was a manifestation of a universal dynamic in relationship that goes beyond the bedroom. It is the "advance and retreat" phenomenon. It is common for one partner to advance in order to come closer to the other, and that very advance causes the other to retreat. When one person in the system takes a polar position, the other has a tendency to move toward the opposite pole, unconsciously working to keep the system in a state of balance. This phenomenon can be generalized beyond intimate relationships, and can even be found in the cold halls of the business world.

I had an organizational client in the publishing business, and was presented with a situation in which the Marketing and Sales Manager was withholding sales information from the Chief Operating Officer. She was doing so because she was not satisfied with her own performance, not having reached her stated sales goals. Given "a bit more time," she felt she would. The more Dolores struggled to withhold and protect her data, the more Allan pushed to get it. The more Allan pushed, the more Dolores withdrew into secrecy. This dance put their day-to-day working relationship in jeopardy, and locked them into a counterclockwise cycle that satisfied neither. Both ended up not feeling good about themselves or the other.

We achieved a breakthrough at an organizational retreat with a similar kind of role reversal intervention that helped Liz and Bill get out of their stuck place. In this case it involved a manufacturing company I worked with. Sales was not communicating openly with Production, and Production was pushing for more information. As the Production Manager pushed, the Sales Manager withdrew. From an altitude of 10,000 feet above the fray, the interaction between these two would have looked very much like Bill and Liz's sexual dance. So, though we tend to see the sexual component of our lives as unique and separate from other relationship dynamics, in reality the former is like a photographic image of the latter.

At the individual level also, sexual dysfunction is often a symptom of an unrecognized emotional issue manifested in physical form. I had a client named Phil who came to see me because he often couldn't get an erection when his wife wanted to make love. They both were frustrated, and it was becoming a block to their overall intimacy. They had an otherwise happy relationship, communicated well, and felt they had tried everything under the sun on the physical level, but the erectile dysfunction remained.

When Phil and I worked together, he went deeply into his feelings. He discovered that although it had been a long time since his divorce from his previous wife, he had not fully grieved the pain he had experienced as a result of it. Phil had left his wife for the woman he was presently with. But the pain of the family breakup, the pain of disconnection, and the difficulty it caused for his children still throbbed unconsciously beneath the surface. Unawares, Phil was bringing this pain into the bedroom with him, which interfered with his ability to get an erection. As Phil saw and understood this, he cried the tears for, and grieved the loss of, what had been. He subsequently became more available for his present sexual relationship. In Phil's case, the outcome of going underneath the apparent physical issue to the underlying emotional cause was a great victory. He no longer had a problem getting an erection, and is now having wonderful sex with the woman he dearly loves.

Sex, among other things, is a form of play for adults. For that reason it is sometimes helpful to treat it playfully, especially as a short-run measure to help break a counterclockwise cycle. Approach what has become heavy and super-serious more lightly, loosely, and with the flexibility children take to their fun. Being more playful also helps us get away from trying to match an inappropriate, culture-bound image of how it is "supposed to be," and to go more with the current of what it actually is. The sexual component of a couple's life is not the place to make a stand. In play we cooperate; we don't dig our heels in to have it our way. The sexual realm is not the place to "prove" that we are independent or to create artificial boundaries to compensate for a lack in the rest of the relationship. It's best to make those shifts first in the other aspects of the relationship, and to allow the sexual sphere to be more lighthearted. We play best with friends who are equals. If both partners are truly friends and equals, then sex is likely to be excellent.

Tom and Nancy were experiencing sexual difficulties. They decided to take the playful approach to breaking the counterclockwise cycle and reconnecting. They had a few drinks and did some role-playing. Tom left the house and came to the door as a stranded motorist. Nancy opened the door looking quite sexy in a skimpy robe. Nancy played at reluctantly letting Tom into the house to make a phone call. Once in, Tom proceeded to seduce her. They had a wonderful time, and some of the heaviness that had plagued them faded away. They later played a similar game with Tom in the role of a census-taker, who again seduced Nancy. This playfulness and lightness really helped the couple get out of their rut, turn the clock in the right direction, and open them up to addressing the deeper emotional issues that were getting in the way in the first place.

Another doorway to sexual healing is for partners to get into bed naked, with the agreement that they will not have intercourse. They talk, touch, and behave as sexually as each partner is open to, without intercourse. This is particularly good when one partner feels pressured or is having trouble opening. It takes the pressure off that person and allows opening to happen at its own pace, more naturally, in an unforced way. Later, a verbal agreement can be made as to when and where to get naked and take the connection to intercourse. Making explicit agreements about when and where helps a partner who is not feeling open to experience less pressure at other times. It allows that person not to be stuck in the retreat mode. It also assures the other partner, who is frustrated that sex is too infrequent, that it will happen, and exactly when.

Over the years, in discussions about this intimate subject, many women have told me that for them talk is an important form of foreplay. This information is not in the realm of many men's thoughts. So to support a non-pressured connection, it is good to go into conversation before going into physical connection. It allows your partner to feel more trusting, open, and ready to be vulnerable in the way that sex demands.

In short, if we are willing to expand our self-awareness, the challenge of sex—like the other challenges relationship provides—is an opportunity for growth and healing in our lives both separately and together. In the words of Kathleen Winsor, "Sex is something big and cosmic. What else do we have? There's only birth and death and the union of two people—and sex is the only one that happens to us more than once."

18 ❧ Children, Money, and Chores

The hand that rocks the cradle rules the world.

FOLK SAYING

*I*n *addition* to sex, children, money, and chores are among the most common issues around which couples get stuck. When Barbara and I speak about the couples groups we conduct, we often mention, tongue in cheek, that couples work is more straightforward than individual work, because all couples fight over the same things: sex, children, money, and domestic duties.

For many couples, adjusting in a healthy way to the impact of children on a relationship is extremely challenging, and of central importance in the art of sustaining intimacy. For me, my daughter has been one of the greatest joys in my life. And as a parent, I also see how tough on intimacy the introduction of children can be to a relationship. The most significant challenge is maintaining the adult-to-adult connection as the top priority, while at the same time being loving, responsible parents. It is almost universal in the literature on family systems that the healthiest approach to parenting, both for our children and ourselves, is to give primacy to the adult-to-adult bond. Yet many, I dare say *most*, couples, once they become parents, slip into an almost total focus on the children. They allow the adult-to-adult relationship to become secondary. Secondary does not sustain intimacy. The family itself can be threatened by this generally unconscious shift in priorities and attention. Due to their beauty, magnetism, vulnerability, and need for our full attention, children easily become a focus for all our energy and affection. But if we capitulate to that, the food that feeds the adult-to-adult union is absent, and the relationship is starved of intimacy.

Unfortunately, the moral high ground approach is to "take care of the kids first." And many couples do, sacrificing over time the quality of their own connection. For some, the diversion of full attention to the children is a conscious or unconscious strategy to avoid dealing with the challenges of adult relationship. With a breakdown in the quality of the bond between partners, the modeling for the children is diminished, and the family system is reduced to a lower level of emotional health. However, if we continue nourishing our relationship while we nurture our children, we will have the necessary support, energy, and enthusiasm for both parenting and intimacy.

The working couples we see often tell us that there are too many demands on their lives, with work and children, to take time for each other. Yet, they express a longing for intimacy with their partner. Certainly couples with young children have more time challenges than couples without children, or those whose nests have already emptied. But what does it really mean to say "we don't have enough time for each other"? We all have the exact same amount of time. We all have 24/7. We each choose, or allow to be chosen for us, how we allot that time.

Of course, when our children's vital needs are calling us, we must meet them, diminishing the amount of time we have choice over. Still, we all, at some level, have choice about how to use the majority of our hours in the day. And we make our choices based on either an examined or unexamined set of priorities. We are not mere victims of the clock. If we choose to be both parents and top dogs at work, then we are choosing that and its consequences for relationship. If we are choosing to be parents and the fittest dog in the gym, then we are choosing that and its consequences for relationship. Whatever we choose, the allocation of our time is our decision, and it has observable consequences in our lives.

If we want our kids to play soccer and basketball and we choose to drive them to practice five days a week, then that is our choice, as well as its consequence. We have made that decision and elected its outcome for our relationship. If we take the time to make our house spotlessly clean, then we are choosing that and its consequences. No decree, as of yet, has been issued about how we spend our time.

After children arrive, choosing to continue to make the adult-to-adult relationship a top priority, and to distribute our time so that we sustain and nourish it, is the key to maintaining intimacy. And ultimately, to being loving parents.

Childrearing

Skillful childrearing practices can be very supportive of adult-to-adult intimacy. When we understand and implement the skills that help our children behave cooperatively, it makes it easier to jump this hurdle.

The main skill that helped in raising my daughter was developing an open and honest communication channel between us. As the adult in this relationship, this was my responsibility; I could not expect that process to begin with her. Unfortunately, the opposite assumption, usually unexamined, is prevalent. We expect our children to be open and honest about their behavior and feelings with us, even when we are not equally open and honest with them. Why would we expect our children to learn such behavior without modeling it ourselves?

When my daughter was about seven years old, I noticed that when I inquired about her school experience or her friends, I would inevitably get the same one syllable answer: "Fine." After much frustration, I decided to experiment with the basic communication skills that work well in adult relationships. We model with our behavior what we want from the other. I began to speak about myself openly and honestly to her. Instead of asking about her schooling and how she was feeling about it, I would tell her about my workday and how I was feeling about it. Instead of asking about her friends and how she was feeling about them, I would tell her about my friends and how I was feeling about them. It worked! Before long she began to do the same with me. By positive modeling, rather than nagging, she learned a new way to communicate. She saw my behavior as the normal way one communicates. She began to share more fully with me the contents of her life.

As my daughter became an adolescent, with the challenges of sex, smoking, drinking, drugs, and all the potential risks in our present society, I found I could not just make rules and expect her to mindlessly follow them. We did set limits and boundaries, but more importantly, I spoke to her from my heart about how I felt regarding the dangers she was facing. I told her that what I would like is for her to hear me out fully. She didn't have to agree with me. Just listen attentively to my feelings on these matters. Then to go forward using her own best judgment, making her own choices in each situation. The idea was not to demand that she behave in a certain way, a strategy I saw failing all around me. It was to inform her, and to count on the goodwill generated by that approach, along with the innate desire a child has to please her parents when she is not pushed into rebelliousness by authoritarian methods. Again, it worked! Instead of being cut off or tuned out, I was included in a good deal of her life and decision-making. My daughter listened fully, shared a great deal, and went forward, making, for the most part, responsible and self-loving choices.

Now when we get together in her adulthood, the relationship flows beautifully. We talk and share freely, and sometimes endlessly. We enjoy each other's company enormously. Beyond her innate good nature, I attribute our relationship to having had open and honest communication with her since childhood.

Another, more traditional, approach to childrearing has also helped us. While the child needs her freedom, she also needs to learn how to navigate in society so as not to create a lot of difficult-to-handle backlash. This means teaching her what is traditionally called "manners": habits of social behavior that are considerate and create goodwill. Habits such as being respectful, and saying "please" and "thank you," have helped my daughter integrate more easily into society, and have made her life flow a bit more easily than the lives of children whose parents never bothered to focus on these things.

Money

Like the issue of children, excessive concerns about money in a relationship can become a diversion of focus and a significant block to intimacy.

Even though most middle class families have sufficient means to meet their needs, the high priority given to the acquisition of more material goods often produces a preoccupation that propels money to the top of the priority list. When money becomes the top priority for one partner and not the other, conflict inevitably ensues. When both partners make it top priority, yet another variety of trouble—lack of focus on the relationship—happens.

Like parenting, money can be a trickster by luring one into assuming the moral high ground: "It's for the good of the family." This may appear honorable, but what kind of family will we be taking care of if we are not attending to our primary relationship? What kind of family will we be taking care of if we let the focus on acquisition create a wall between us and our partner? Most likely a family that is dysfunctional and unhappy.

When money becomes a wedge between partners, it is sometimes because one of the partners has historically-based emotional wounding around the issue of money. I am working with a couple right now, Jane and Kenny, who are in this predicament. In their words, they are "madly in love." They look very happy and can't stop touching and kissing. However, Jane broke off the relationship at one point because Kenny "is not responsible around money," meaning, "he doesn't make enough."

Kenny is a gifted artist who paints his abstracts at night, and does construction work during the day to earn a more dependable income. Neither activity has caused him to miss a meal or leave a bill unpaid. In discussing the issue, what soon became apparent is that because Jane had the responsibility of raising four children from a previous marriage, she has a good deal of fear around issues of survival. When she understood that her real concern about money was not Kenny's lack, but her own fear about having enough, she started to withdraw her projection and gradually began to take the pressure off of Kenny. Interestingly, as the pressure came off, Kenny—of his own accord—embarked on the development of an art-related business that appears to have a good chance of financial success.

Though we all must responsibly attend to earning the money we need for ourselves and our family, we don't want the desire for more money to obstruct our relationship. If we do, the whole house of cards may some day come tumbling down. We will be sitting with our worldly goods all around us, but have no family or partner to enjoy them with.

Chores, Tidiness, and Timeliness

There are other, more mundane, but ever-present issues that each of has an idiosyncratic relationship to, like doing chores, tidiness, and timeliness. These, too, can be bones of contention between partners. If conflict around these mundane matters becomes chronic, it can seriously undermine intimacy.

In domestic life, there are basic things that need to be taken care of in order to maintain a healthy home environment. Food needs to be cooked, dishes have to be washed, the house has to be cleaned, light bulbs must be changed, and so on. Who does what, when, how often, and how well can either be a source of satisfying teamwork, or a cause for friction.

Traditional gender roles, though breaking down substantially, still have a hold on many of us in the deep layers of our unconscious. We may believe in them or oppose them, but somehow their influence remains. In some cases, though the woman in a couple may be working at her job every bit as diligently as the man, they both may have the unexamined belief that it is she who is more responsible for the domestic chores. Similarly, we may hold the unexamined expectation that the man needs to do the "manly things" around the house, like fixing the broken faucet and mowing the lawn. Yet for any specific couple, this arrangement may not fit each partner's skills or desires. It is important that, to whatever extent possible, these unconscious beliefs be examined and brought to consciousness so that the partners can openly choose together the division of labor that suits their unique needs. They can explicitly negotiate and come to clear agreements about who does what.

So, for example, we may agree that if you cook, I wash the dishes. If I cook, you wash the dishes. If I am working that day and you are not, you do both, and vice versa. I will take on more responsibility for paying bills, and you will take on more for cleaning the house, and so on. If the domestic division of labor is clearly negotiated, then when someone is not upholding their end of the agreement, it can be dealt with cleanly. If the division of labor is ill-defined and based only on unexamined and undiscussed assumptions, then when dissatisfaction arises, the discussion is likely to degenerate into personal criticism.

I have noticed in these times of greater gender equality that there has developed what appears to me to be an unhelpfully strict standard around equality in childrearing that does not serve the intimacy of the couple. The assumption is that each parent must spend the exact same amount of time in childcare duties. I have often seen mothers focus first on handing off the kids to dad when he comes home, before even greeting him, because it is "his turn." But dad wants to be received in a loving, supportive way by his intimate partner. In that moment he feels a wall go up between himself and his partner. Over time, this erodes the connection. It is far better to focus on supporting, helping, and connecting with one another than on keeping a timesheet and scorecard.

Two other areas of domestic life that often cause chronic strife are timeliness and tidiness. Each of us has different standards and habits around these matters. Somehow we want—even expect—the other to share our standards and habits around these quite personal and idiosyncratic preferences. If I want to be scrupulously punctual in every instance, and my partner is more relaxed and casual about it, we may have a problem. It would not be unusual to fight about it, and for each of us to fill up a bag of resentment because of it. There can be a similar dynamic around the issue of tidiness. One partner may hold a high standard regarding what it means for the house to be clean, while the other may have a more care-free attitude. The former is uncomfortable if things are not put away and the house spotless, while the latter enjoys a creative mess.

What to do? Based on the principle of not trying to change the other, we need to focus on ourselves. If we cannot find a way to resolve this difference amicably, then I need to find a way to be on time and let my partner take care of herself. If I need the house to be spotlessly clean, then I must take responsibility for keeping it so. In neither case is it useful to criticize my partner or start a fight, which at base arises from the obvious and universal fact that each of us is different.

As an alternative to ascending our high horse about the correctness of our position, we need to understand that our position is no better or worse than our partner's. It is simply our position, the one we prefer. Our standards and needs are just as likely to originate from an equally idiosyncratic place as our partner's. A solution that demands the other to change is not a real solution. While tidiness seems to hold the moral high ground, one's desire for it may just as easily originate in the fear of disorder as from a positive, healthful perspective. While promptness holds the higher moral ground, one's need to be on time may originate in fear as well, rooted in a history of having been punished for being late. In these commonplace matters, we need to put the quality of our relationship above our idiosyncrasies. We will be more content and at peace with a happy relationship than with making it to the party on time with an unhappy partner. Due to the destructiveness these small matters can generate, it is not wise to force our preferences on our true companion.

In one workshop, we dove into a participating couple's chronic friction around timeliness. They arrived late to the evening session, and the man complained to the group of his discomfort with his wife around this issue. Instead of treating the matter as a distraction for the group, we helped them explore their process.

Underneath Arnold's anger at Helena for her chronic tardiness was a projection process. He himself had the tendency to be late, and had to push himself hard to be punctual. As he observed Helena's relaxed attitude, resentment and self-judgment came up, and he put that negativity on Helena. For her part, Helena felt she was carrying an unduly heavy load about a relatively unimportant matter. And she was, since most of the baggage was Arnold's, offloaded onto her. Still, Helena was willing to explore her part of the equation. What she discovered was an unconscious rebellious attitude, which actually drove her not to follow generally accepted rules, in this case, the expectations about timeliness. She was not going to conform to any guideline she did not participate in making. Inquiring even more deeply, she saw that due to her low self-esteem, she did not see herself as mattering to other people. Unconsciously, she felt that it was not important to the people on the other end of the engagement whether she was there or not.

Once they recognized their own emotional patterns and attachments, Arnold and Helena lightened up on their judgment and criticism of each other. Timeliness became a more straightforward logistical problem to solve, devoid of emotional content. And they were happier for it.

19 ❧ The Seven Virtues

The following is a model for relationship I developed in the book *Jupiter's Rings: Balance From the Inside Out.*[11] It is a prescription for a healthy intimate partnership, based on developing and enacting the following seven virtues:

1. *Awareness*

2. *Truth*

3. *Acceptance*

4. *Expression*

5. *Intuition*

6. *Intention*

7. *Non-attachment to outcome*

These elements unfold sequentially, one leading to the next, with a developmental logic:

awareness > truth > acceptance > expression
> intuition > intention > non-attachment

The seven virtues can be grouped into the three basic components of relationship-building: *Owning, Sharing,* and *Context for Action.*

The first three elements, *Awareness, Truth,* and *Acceptance,* constitute the *Owning* component of the Healing Relationship. Owning means to take responsibility for one's own truth and feelings. It is a skillful alternative to our more habitual tendency toward judging and blaming others, and denying our own truth.

The fourth virtue, *Expression*, corresponds to the *Sharing* component. It means communicating the truth of our thoughts and feelings to others. Sharing our inner experience, perhaps more than any other single factor, creates intimacy between people. Those with whom we share feel we have bestowed the gift of ourselves upon them; through knowing us better, they are more willing to receive us with welcome.

The final three virtues, *Intuition, Intention,* and *Non-attachment,* make up the *Context for Action.* Together, these elements create the conditions under which our behavior becomes more skillful, effective, and supportive of ourselves and our relationship.

Owning

First, there must be *Awareness.* Before anything else, we need to be observant of what is actually happening in the internal and external environment. We need to be cognizant of ourselves and others, and of what is happening between us, before real connection takes place.

Second, it is necessary to recognize as much as possible about the *Truth* of the moment we are observing: the reality of what is happening in the present, unmitigated by our desire, clinging, or rejection. We try to see what is simply so within ourselves and between us. Otherwise, we are operating with false information in the Never-Never Land of how we want it to be, rather than how it is.

Third, it is necessary to *Accept* the truth of what is, whether we like it or not. Whether it is pleasant or unpleasant, we need to accept the truth of the moment. If we reject or deny it, relationship, intimacy, and effective action do not flourish.

Sharing

Expression is significant because after seeing and accepting the truth within and without, communicating that truth deepens our relationship.

It releases tension for the individual doing the expressing, and thereby helps us be more present for the interaction. Expression connects us to the listener by creating the kind of intimacy that comes only through sharing our self with them.

Context For Action

Intuition is our greatest resource for moving toward skillful action. When we know and accept the truth of our inner and outer circumstances, then connect through expression, intuition becomes our best guide for effective behavior. From intuition emerges understanding and guidance for our next appropriate steps.

Intention defines and points us in the direction we wish to go. Intention is very important because it generates the power of purpose. In relationship, intention asks that we come to agreement about shared goals, and maximizes the potential to achieve them together. Without intention, we may simply wander about the countryside and never arrive at our destination.

Non-attachment, though it is the paradoxical element in the Healing Relationship model, is paramount. The first six factors set up the possibility of a satisfying relationship. The seventh, an attitude of non-attachment, requires that we do not cling to that outcome. We remain open to all possibilities, accepting all outcomes as permissible, without struggling or squeezing anything into submission.

The ability to be open to outcome, the willingness to accept what is, does not constitute a lack of caring. Rather, it is simple humility. It is acknowledging the truth that we are not in control of the universe, and being wise enough to gratefully receive whatever it brings us. The core of the non-attachment paradox is that it creates the highest probability that the outcome we desire will, in fact, happen. It is *giving up to get our way*. Non-attachment is a highly evolved stance that requires considerable practice to embody in our life.

All seven virtues need to be operative to manifest a superior intimate relationship: first, within our self in relationship to our self, and then within our self in relationship to others. We cannot successfully apply principles to relationships with others that we do not first apply to our relationship with our self.

Living the seven virtues adds up to a powerful quality called "*Presence.*" Presence is communicated by our bearing, and results in others feeling comfort and safety in our company. It brings out the very best in others. Presence is a quality that cannot be captured in words, but that we have all experienced in the fellowship of special people.

To turn an aphorism on its head, "virtue is *more than* its own reward." I do not advocate cultivating these seven virtues because they are good, moral, or right. I advocate them because they work. They are wonderful allies in constructing a harmonious relationship and balanced life.

For the most part, sincere action produces sincere reaction. Likewise, insincere action produces insincere reaction. Emphasizing the seven virtues in our relationship with others will be reflected back to us in the quality of our connectedness. Our partner will feel more comfortable in our presence. She will be more open to sharing the truth of her own experience with us; perhaps he will even feel safe enough to express his deeper feelings. Not always, and not necessarily, of course, but in the long run it will deepen, enrich, and enliven our relationships as a whole. I have seen the magic of applying the seven virtues to building relationships and nourishing intimacy. It works!

20❧ There Is No Need for War

When a man has made peace within himself,
he will be able to make peace in the whole world.
RABBI BUNAM

The principles that create intimate relationship are also the principles that build peace. If we do the personal work that produces peace within, and the relationship work that develops intimacy, then we have learned to be an instrument of peace. As the great teacher of nonviolence, Mahatma Gandhi, said, "If you want peace, be peace."

If our national and international leaders were to do their personal emotional and spiritual work, then communication and love would become the natural and righteous alternative to war. The parallel between individual peacemaking and international peacemaking can be seen in the military maxim, "it is easy to start a war, but hard to end it." In interpersonal relations, it is easy to start a fight with our partner out of unconscious motives and a lack of owning the source of our own reactivity, but it is hard to end the conflict once it has begun its negative counterclockwise dive toward division. Just as wars have profound negative effects long after open hostilities have ceased, unskillful interpersonal fighting creates a legacy of resentment long after the actual fighting has ended. It is generally accepted by historians that the primary cause of World War II was the unskillful and punitive resolution of World War I. Likewise, much of the horror in the Middle East today is a result of the atrocities of WWII. Similarly, many conflicts in couples are not really over the present material about which they appear to be fighting, but about previous unresolved conflicts that have embittered the partners.

I knew a couple whose chronic fighting mode became so serious that they were on the brink of divorce. In therapy, after much haggling and one-upsmanship, the woman finally confessed that she had never forgiven her husband for not expressing happiness when she had informed him that she was pregnant with their third child. This lack of owning the source of her own reactivity, and the lack of communication between her and her partner, contributed substantially to many years of conflict and their eventual divorce.

Peace in relationship, as in international affairs, is not so much about stopping hostilities as creating the conditions under which there does not have to be war. The most recent large-scale American wars, in Vietnam and Iraq, are examples of the lack of basic personal and interpersonal development on the part of the leaders who launched them. We got into these conflicts due to reactivity and unexamined motives. In the case of Vietnam, it was an irrational and misplaced fear of communism; in the case of Iraq, an unexamined fear of terrorism and the lust for vengeance stemming from the horror of the attacks of September 11, 2001. We had an enormously difficult time getting out of Vietnam. At present, we are having an equally difficult time extricating ourselves from Iraq. Both wars have produced long-term negative repercussions and trauma that will cloud the future of international relations, peace, and the lives of thousands upon thousands of people for a very long time.

As in personal matters, the power of apology goes a long way toward generating the reconciliation necessary to bring these consequences to an end—an apology in the form of owning one's part in producing the conflict and sincerely expressing remorse for its consequences. When it comes to interpersonal affairs, I have been amazed at how much healing comes from one person in the relationship owning the source of his reactivity and sharing it, along with an expression of regret.

I experienced a dramatic example of this as a participant in a group psychological exercise. With the help of a skilled facilitator, we reenacted the meeting between a woman in the group and her rapist. I played the part of the rapist, with the intention of healing the trauma. As I felt my way into the role, my authentic feeling was a deep remorse for causing this woman so much pain. With tears in my eyes and a cracking voice, I apologized for my behavior and its effect on her. The woman began to weep, and continued to cry for a long time. She later reported that these were tears of relief and release that she had so longed for, but had never experienced, despite all the previous psychological work she had done on this issue. An apology from the person portraying her perpetrator turned out to be the most healing therapy for this deep trauma.

At the international level, Reconciliation Commissions, such as the one in South Africa, have proven the same principle. When perpetrators come forward to admit guilt, apologize for their actions, and request forgiveness, healing at the national level becomes possible.

Dealing skillfully with anger is central to peacemaking. While most of those who teach about anger and peace advise some sort of suppression of anger, this is not the most skillful means. The best approach to transforming anger into a positive force is truly feeling one's way into the anger without acting it out. Not suppressing the feeling will only cause it to arise later in some unexpected and harmful way. Doing the Emotional Wisdom work necessary to leech out the harmful consequences and draw out its positive lessons is the most graceful and peaceful way to master anger.

Yelling at a loved one or throwing a plate through the kitchen window is not a good approach to anger management, because it is likely to engender the counterclockwise spiral. On the other hand, screaming into a pillow or smashing a plastic bat on the bed—neither of which harms another or creates a cycle of negative actions—will release the bodily component of anger and bring relief, without the detrimental consequences.

Anger is a powerful source of energy. If we learn to resource anger, to tap into its essential energy in order to fuel constructive action, but without acting out harmful behavior, then we can make anger an ally and an instrument of peace.

Learning how to communicate anger is also a challenge. Releasing it on another by yelling and screaming just makes things worse; sensing one's way into the anger and communicating the feeling behind it supports peace, not war.

Similarly, the strong need to be right, so alive within us, is a force we must learn to manage if we are to have peace at the microscopic and macroscopic levels. Developing our self emotionally and spiritually creates a secure place within us that erases the need to find safety by being right through making the other person wrong. This comes from the personal growth that emerges out of a self-inquiry process.

Peace is a choice. We can choose to stay with our anger and let it drive our behavior; we can choose to be right, no matter the consequences, letting it destroy the goodwill in our relationship. Or, we can choose peace.

Similarly, our national leaders can choose to look strong and maintain their power by appealing to a primitive level of consciousness, or they can choose the more courageous path of dedication to communication and peacemaking.

For peace we must learn to look for what is right in the other's position and find a way to honor it, rather than focusing exclusively on what is wrong with the other's position and emphasizing difference and division. It is possible to stand up for our self *and* choose peace at the same time. We can set limits as to what we will accept and not accept, and keep communication as our tool of choice. Or, we can sink into the macho approach to interpersonal and international relations, relying on weapons of destruction, and fail. The macho way is about pushing other people into doing what we want them to do, and making our self feel good by exercising force and intimidation. The peaceful way is to value our self enough that we do not need to coerce others in order to gain self-respect.

In the words of Henning Mankell, "War is always a mistake. Or, the result of absurd assumptions and conclusions."

21 ❧ A Summary of Principles

- Most psychological work is about freeing our self from conditioned restriction, and opening up into expansiveness: experiencing freedom in feeling, thought, and action, which allows us to be in the present.

- Most relationship work is about freeing our self from conditioned restriction, and opening up into expansiveness in the presence of another.

- Most of our reactivity to our intimate partner stems from seeing in them parts of our self that we have rejected.

- Much of our reactivity to our partner stems from trying to prove to them, but really to our self, that we are worthy.

- Much of the suffering in relationship comes from trying to change the other, or to make them different from who and what they are.

- The way out of relationship constriction is acceptance of our self and the other exactly as we and they are.

Guidelines for a Happy Relationship

- Ask for what you want, and don't expect to get it.

- Healthy change comes from the other as a gift, not from coercion.

- If you don't like something, don't try to change the other. Change yourself.

- Be kind to your partner, even when you're not in the mood.

- Communicate a lot. Way more than you think necessary.

Endnotes

[1]Although I have written this book from the perspective of my experience as a heterosexual male in a long-term intimate relationship with a woman, I have found in working with same-sex couples that the relationship dynamics are similar to those of heterosexual couples. I therefore think the *principles* outlined here apply equally well to both types of relationship. Accordingly, my hope is that intimate partners in general, regardless of their sexual orientation, will find this book useful.

[2]Gendlin's approach is detailed in his book *Focusing* (Bantam, 1981).

[3]"Sunbeams," in *The Sun* (2002).

[4]A.H. Almaas, *What Really Matters* (Bantam Books, 1995), p. 406.

[5]"Buttering the Sky," from *The Gift: Poems by Hafiz, The Great Sufi Master*, Trans. Daniel Ladinsky (Penguin Compass, 1999), p. 300.

[6]Viktor Frankl, *Man's Search for Meaning* (Washington Square Press, 1964).

[7]John Firman, *The Primal Wound: A Transpersonal View of Trauma, Addiction, and Growth* (State University of New York, 1997).

[8]*The Sun* (August, 2000).

[9]Robert A. Johnson, *Owning Your Own Shadow* (HaperOne, 1993).

[10]John Steinbeck IV, Nancy Steinbeck, and Andrew Harvey, *The Other Side of Eden: Life with John Steinbeck* (Prometheus, 2001), p. 169.

[11]Howard Schechter, *Jupiter's Rings: Balance from the Inside Out* (White Cloud Press, 2002).

About the Author

HOWARD JOEL SCHECHTER, PH.D. is the author of *Rekindling the Spirit in Work* and *Jupiter's Rings: Balance From the Inside Out*. He works as a teacher, consultant, counselor, and artist. He is an Honors Graduate of the University of Michigan, and received his doctorate in sociology from Northwestern University in Evanston, Illinois. He is a longtime workshop leader at Esalen Institute in Big Sur, California, and other venues around the nation and the world. He has served as an organization consultant for 30 years, helping corporate, private, and non-profit groups improve the human side of their enterprise.

Howard can be contacted at Howardjoel@rekindling.com.

CPSIA information can be obtained at www.ICGtesting.com
Printed in the USA
LVOW08s1036211013

357812LV00002B/60/P

9 781581 771091